Surviving Your Preschooler

Surviving Your Preschooler

365 Creative Games and Activities to occupy Your Three- to Six-Year-old

TRISH KUFFNER

Lighthouse Books
1423 Dayton Street
Coquitlam, B.C. Canada
V3E 3H2

Cover and interior design by Ruth Linka
Illustrations by Sheila Manning Kinakin

First printing, October, 1998

CANADIAN CATALOGUING IN PUBLICATION DATA

Kuffner, Patricia, 1960-
Surviving your preschooler

Includes bibliographical references and index.
ISBN 0-9696626-1-0

1. Creative activities and seat work. 2. Amusements. I. Title.
LB1140.35.   C74K83 1998   649'.5   C98-910917-8

PRINTED IN CANADA BY WEBCOM

For my husband, Wayne,
and our four precious children,
Andria, Emily, Joshua, and Johanna.

I have learned far more from you
than you will ever learn from me.

Table of Contents

Acknowledgements

The production of a book is no small job, and I could not have done it without the help of so many wonderful people.

First and foremost, I must thank "Nana", Betty Kuffner, and "Grandma", Irene McGeorge. They are always ready and willing to lend a hand and help out with the children when I need time to write or tend to other aspects of the business. Your support of my efforts is invaluable.

A great, big "thank-you" also goes to my husband, Wayne, and our children, Andria, Emily, Joshua, and Johanna. When Mom gets busy, clean laundry and decent meals are put on hold so that "the book" can take priority. I deeply appreciate the sacrifices you've made, as well as all the help you've given me hauling, stickering, packing, and shipping books over the past six years.

Self-publishing is a wonderful venture, but one with a very distinct drawback – what to do when hundreds of boxes of books arrive from the printer! Thank-you to Barry and Karen Kinakin, and Jack and Irene McGeorge, who, at one time or another, have had thousands of books stored in their basements. I appreciate the trouble you have gone to on my behalf.

Finally, thank-you to the thousands of parents and caregivers across Canada who purchased the first edition of *Surviving Your Preschooler*. I would not be publishing a second edition were it not for your support. I am extremely grateful to each and every one of you, and especially to those who have taken the time to write to me over the years. Your encouragement makes it all worthwhile.

Introduction

If I had My Child to Raise Over Again

If I had my child to raise over again,
I'd fingerpaint more and point the finger less.
I'd do less correcting and more connecting.
I'd take my eyes off my watch, and watch with my eyes.
I would care to know less and know to care more.
I'd take more hikes and fly more kites.
I'd stop playing serious, and seriously play.
I'd run through more fields and gaze at more stars.
I'd do more hugging and less tugging.
I would be firm less often, and affirm much more.
I'd build self-esteem first, and the house later.
I'd teach less about the love of power, and more about the power of love.

DIANE LOOMANS

I BRAVELY BEGAN WRITING THIS BOOK IN 1992, IN THE MIDST OF A PER-sonal parenting crisis. It was an exceptionally rainy British Columbia winter. Andria, my oldest daughter, was three. Her sister Emily was almost two, and baby Joshua was not yet six months old. Emily was in the midst of toilet training, and Josh nursed at least every two hours. Andria, normally sweet-tempered and easy-to-please, was becoming very hard to deal with. As the rain continued, her moodiness increased. She needed new things to do, new experiences, but most of my time and energy went into meeting the needs of the two younger ones. As the days dragged on and frustration festered, I entertained a multitude of doubts

1

about my ability (or lack thereof) to be a good mother. I had always heard about "quality time" with your child; I seemed to have an abundance of quantity time without much quality!

While I knew I couldn't always expect to drop everything to get involved with her, I knew there must be something I could do to provide my preschooler with a more creative and stimulating environment. I knew there must be activities that would both challenge and entertain. I wanted ideas for little projects we could work on together, but I also wanted things she could do on her own while I was busy elsewhere. Since we were living on one income, I also needed activities that made use of basic items we already had around the house.

I started to reorganize our home to better meet the changing needs of our family. I began collecting and saving all kinds of interesting things that we could use in our activities. I became much more organized and tried to plan for special things we could do together. I also relaxed a little and learned to take my responsibilities as a parent less seriously. I learned to enjoy my children and their small and simple pleasures. Confidence in my parenting abilities returned as I began to feel in control again. And that's when the idea for *Surviving Your Preschooler* began to take root.

Six years have now passed since *Surviving Your Preschooler* was first published. Since then, more than 20,000 copies have been sold in Canada alone. Looking back, it seems that it was a bit presumptuous of me to use the word "surviving" in the title, when I had not yet survived the preschool years myself! But I realize now that had I waited until my own children were out of the preschool stage to write the book, it would not likely have been written in such a way as to become the valuable resource that it is. My experiences at home, all day, every day, with three very young children, taught me much about what works and what doesn't. Being able to make up or evaluate crafts, games and activities with my own built-in test panel gave me the invaluable feedback I needed in choosing the best and most practical ideas for this book. Thinking through what I needed at the time, and how I would like it organized, led me to put together a resource that thousands of others across the country have found so helpful.

This revised edition of *Surviving Your Preschooler* is a compilation of the ideas and activities that met my needs as a parent, as well as the needs of my children, during those challenging preschool years. It contains suggestions for every situation and occasion, for both indoors and out, for summer and winter, for the quiet times and the not-so-quiet ones. Although this book may be written by a stay-at-home mom as a resource for others in the same situation, be assured that it is well-suited for anyone who has a preschooler in their life, be it mothers or fathers, grandparents, aunts or uncles, babysitters, daycare workers, preschool teachers, church workers, or playgroup leaders. If you are looking for one good book on what to do with a preschooler and how to do it, this book is indeed for you.

While many ideas in this book will continue to entertain your children long after the preschool stage, the activities in this book are most suitable for children between the ages of three and six. Because there is such a difference in the abilities of children in that age range, some ideas will be too advanced for a three-year-old, while others will be too simple for a five- or six-year-old. Use your own judgement in choosing activities that best meet the capabilities and interests of your own child and be prepared to supervise when necessary.

A note on the use of "his" and "her"; in recognition of the fact that children do indeed come in both genders, and in order not to show preference for either, the use of the male and female pronouns will alternate with each chapter.

Yes, I did survive the preschool years. Our three oldest children are now ten, eight and seven. Revising this book has been a wonderful experience, helping me to remember many of the fun times we had and some of the special things we did together during those precious preschool years. We have since been blessed with our fourth child, Johanna, now a full-fledged toddler, who will be joined by a baby sister or brother sometime around her second birthday next year. Soon I'll be going through the preschool stage again, but this time with my three older helpers!

Enjoy your preschooler! Although it may seem at times that they will never grow up, they always do. The long, seemingly endless days will gradually be replaced by days with not enough hours in them. Children who once needed you for everything will need you less and less, and the days of leisurely walks, painting, playdough and afternoon naps will be a warm and fuzzy memory. My hope is that both you and your child will have many happy hours of playing, growing and learning together.

PATRICIA KUFFNER, SEPTEMBER, 1998

CHAPTER ONE

Help! I Have a Preschooler!

To be a good housewife and mother, you have to be more self-generated. You have to create your own playground of the imagination, and the mind. To be a really good, creative mother you have to be an extraordinary woman. You have to keep yourself involved with your child during great periods of the day when it's just the two of you and you feel that at any moment you may literally go out of your mind.

MERYL STREEP

PRESCHOOLERS! THEY DON'T EMERGE OVERNIGHT, OR ON THEIR THIRD birthday. It may happen so slowly, you hardly notice it at all, but one day you realize that your clumsy, confusing little toddler is gone. In his place is an energetic, intensely curious, sometimes determined (some might call it stubborn), very adventurous little child. Chances are he is out of diapers, off the bottle, and somewhat able to take a little responsibility for himself. He probably knows the rules of the house, and doesn't need constant monitoring. After a few years of babies and toddlers, parents often find the preschool stage quite refreshing.

But while life with a preschooler can be a celebration, you will always have days when it seems more like a chore. We all have bad days, and children are no exception. Your child may be a wonderful little person most of the time, but his boundless energy and relatively short attention span may result in some irritating, demanding and temperamental behaviour. While providing your child with lots of fun and interesting things to do won't solve all his behaviour problems, it may help prevent some of the signs and symptoms of boredom that result from a lack of appropriate stimulation.

There are many ways to stimulate your child. At around the age of three, children often enter a preschool or playgroup for two or more days a week. A group such as this will usually provide your child with new friends and a new outlet for his creativity and energy. If your child spends all his time at home with you or another caregiver, he relies on you for new experiences, outings and creative activities. His day needs some structure – a loose schedule with recognizable breaks. He needs to meet people of different ages – adults and children alike. He relies on you to introduce him to books and music, arts and crafts projects, rambunctious games, and quiet learning activities. A short walk or some outdoor play should be part of every day.

While a variety of experiences and activities are essential to your child's development, resist the urge to push him too hard. All children need lots of time for creative and spontaneous play. Rather than assuming the role of teacher, instructing and directing your child, try to act as his helper in the learning process. Children need to learn on their own and to run their own show, while knowing that you are there to help them when and if they need it. Children who have learned to direct their own play, who have been given lots of time to be creative and to use their imaginations, are less likely to experience boredom than those whose time has been rigidly planned for them.

"But There's Nothing to do..."

All children, no matter how creative, imaginative and self-sufficient, will at one time or another experience a case of boredom or restlessness. Here are some suggestions to help you alleviate boredom in your preschooler.

KEEP A BAKER'S BOX IN THE KITCHEN

Whether you're in the kitchen a little or a lot, your child will naturally want to be with you when you are. Kitchen cupboards and drawers are full of interesting things that may prove irresistible to your child. Why not provide your child with his very own Baker's Box? Put together a collection of unbreakable kitchen tools in a plastic crate or small storage box. Store it in a spare cupboard that is low enough for your child to reach on his own. He can use his tools for play or for doing some "real" cooking or baking with you. Some suggestions for a Baker's Box are:

cakepan
cake rack
cookie cutters
cookie sheet
large metal or plastic bowl
measuring spoons
muffin tin
pie plate
plastic measuring cups
rubber spatula
wooden spoon

HAVE A BUSY BOX HANDY

A spare kitchen cupboard low enough for your child to reach is an ideal spot for his very own Busy Box. Fill a small storage box or plastic crate with things that he can do on his own, any time he wants. Good things to keep in a Busy Box are:

child-safe scissors
colouring books
construction paper
cookie cutters
crayons
glue
ink pad with ink stamps
paper
playdough
stickers
tape

MAKE UP A RAINY DAY BOX

Although all days with preschoolers can seem long, rainy days seem to have extra hours to fill. When the weather is bad, or when your child is sick, a Rainy Day Box full of surprises can help break the monotony. Good things to stock your Rainy Day Box with are:

- fresh, new art supplies (a new pad, markers, paintbox, stickers, or playdough)
- a new toy (or one that hasn't been played with in awhile)
- a new book, music tape or video
- special dress-up items
- cookie cutters and an untried cookie recipe
- a one-minute timer and ideas for timer games (see Timer Fun, Chapter 2)
- a new board or card game
- supplies and directions for a new craft (preassemble all supplies and store them in a zippered freezer bag in the Rainy Day Box until ready to use)
- a pre-drawn map and prize for an Indoor Treasure Hunt

Don't overuse your Rainy Day Box. Store it away in a safe place and bring it out only when the day seems unusually long.

MAKE A JOB JAR FOR YOUR CHILD

Whether you are a working Mom, an at-home Dad, a loving grandparent or an occasional babysitter, sometimes you will have household chores to do while your preschooler is around. Providing a job jar for your child gives him something to do while you work, and can also help instill a sense of responsibility toward household chores.

You can make a job jar for your child out of an empty jar, coffee can, or small box. Cut strips of paper and on each one print a small job that needs to be done; for example, straighten the book shelves, wash the bathroom sink, put away the towels, wash the vegetables, pick up the toys, and so on. You will know the jobs your child is capable of doing with minimum supervision and assistance. While you do your household chores, have your child pick a job from the job jar. If your child is normally an unwilling helper, allowing him to choose his own job may also help reduce some of his reluctance.

TAKE ALONG A BUSY BAG

Be prepared for those times when you just have to wait—at the doctor's office, at the hairdresser's, or in a restaurant. Turn a drawstring bag or backpack into a take-along Busy Bag that can be filled with special things to keep your child amused. Some suggestions for a Busy Bag are:

- colouring books and paper
- crayons and markers
- dolls and associated clothing, blankets, bottles, and other accessories
- ingredients for an Edible Necklace (see Chapter 5); shoe-string licorice and cereal or crackers with holes in the middle
- magnets and a small metal cake pan (see Magnet Fun, Chapter 5)
- matchbox cars
- puzzles
- special snacks
- stickers and a sticker book

Use your imagination when filling the Busy Bag. Do it yourself, so the contents will be a surprise for your child, or have your child help you fill the bag before you go.

ROTATE YOUR CHILD'S TOYS

In the first few years of life, most children receive many wonderful toys as gifts for birthdays, Christmas, or other occasions. I have always appreciated the good intentions of the givers, but at the same time have been saddened to see such wonderful toys used and played with so rarely. Expensive store-bought toys certainly are nice, but your child will lose interest in even the most creative toys when they are always around. By rotating toys every four to six weeks, they will seem new to him and will be interesting and exciting all over again.

To begin toy rotation, separate your child's toys into piles (if your child has a favourite toy, keep it out all the time). Keep one pile in your child's play area, and pack the others away in boxes, marking on them the dates they are to be brought out. Or if you have good friends with children around the same age as yours, why not try a toy exchange? Keep a list of what has been exchanged, and be sure to agree on the terms of the exchange beforehand (how long, who's responsible for breakage, and so on). This is a great way to find out if that really neat toy your child has his eye on will hold his interest or not!

MAKE A CRAZY CAN

You've probably been there – 5 p.m., dinner nowhere near prepared, a nursing baby in one arm, a cranky toddler hanging onto one leg, and a whiny, demanding preschooler looking for something to do. Now is not the time for fingerpaint or papier-mâché! Now is not the time to brainstorm ideas for exciting and creative things to do with a four-year-old. What you can do is be prepared ahead of time with a Crazy Can.

Make a list of on-the-spot activities that require no special materials, need no time-consuming preparation or clean-up, and above all, demand no large amount of adult participation or supervision. Write down these ideas on index cards or small pieces of paper and place them inside an empty coffee can. (If you like, cover the can with cheerful contact paper, or cover it with plain paper and have your child decorate it with paints, markers, or crayons.) When things start to get crazy (or when there's just "nothing to do"), choose a card from the can for an instant remedy. Appendix B at the back of this book offers a suggested list of activities appropriate for your Crazy Can.

LOOK FOR NEW ACTIVITIES AND EXPERIENCES

While children need free time for creative play, they also rely on you to introduce them to new projects, activities, and adventures. This is hard to do on the spur of the moment, so some advance planning on your part is required. Try to schedule one or two fun, challenging, and creative activities each day (not major projects – sometimes a five-minute game will do!). Decide on the activities ahead of time and have all the necessary supplies assembled in advance. Read on for some additional advice on planning activities for your child.

Planning Your Activities

Failing to plan is planning to fail, and that can apply to the big stuff, like saving for your child's education, as well as the little stuff, like a new art project or playing a game with your child. Recognize the importance of planning new and creative activities. You can have a shelf full of books on activities for children, or just this one, but the ideas this book contains are only valuable to you and your child if you use them (and if you don't do a little advance planning, chances are that you won't use them). Here are some helpful steps for planning your activities.

1. Read this book from cover to cover and fill a weekly planner with activities you would like to try for each day. Include a few alternate activities for when the weather won't cooperate or when things are just not right for what you have planned.

2. Use your weekly activity plan to make a list of supplies you will need, and assemble or purchase them beforehand.

3. Make a list of what you need to prepare before your child becomes involved in the activity – mix paint, draw a treasure hunt map, and so on.

4. Plan special activities for when your child is with a babysitter, and have all the necessary materials handy. This will let your sitter know that a day or night of TV watching is not an option.

5. Make a list of ideas that would be fun to do anytime you can fit them into your schedule. Have this list ready when you have some unexpected free time.

Stocking Your Craft Cupboard

Whether you have a cupboard to spare, or just a box in the basement somewhere, here are some items you should have on hand for the various activities described in this book.

THINGS TO SAVE

aluminum foil • aluminum pie plates (various sizes) • bottle caps • boxes • brown paper bags • buttons • candles • cardboard • catalogues • cereal boxes • chopsticks • clothespins • coffee cans with lids • coins • confetti • corks • cotton balls • cotton batting • cotton swabs • dried beans • dried pasta (different shapes and sizes) • egg cartons • egg shells • empty jars and lids • envelopes • fabric scraps • felt • greeting cards (used) • junk mail • lids from plastic gallon jugs • magazines • metal lids from frozen juice cans • old clothes and costume jewelry for dress-up • old mittens, socks, gloves for puppets • old telephone books • old toothbrushes • paint sample chips • paper clips • paper muffin cup liners • paper plates/cups/bowls • paper scraps • paper towel/toilet paper tubes • photographs of friends and family • pine cones • plastic bowls, lids, bottles • playing cards • popcorn • Popsicle sticks • ribbon • rice (uncooked) • rubber bands • ruler • sandpaper • shoelaces • sponges • spray bottle • stickers of all kinds • string • Styrofoam trays • swizzle sticks • thread • thread spools • toothpicks • wood scraps • wrapping paper scraps • yarn scraps

THINGS TO BUY

art smock (or use an old shirt) • beads • chalk • child-safe scissors • construction paper in various colours • craft magnets • crayons • crepe paper • glitter • glue or glue sticks • googly eyes • hole punch • masking tape • newsprint pads or rolls • paper clips • paper fasteners • pencil crayons • pencil sharpener • pencils • pens • pipe cleaners • plain writing pads • ruler • self-adhesive paper • stapler • stickers • straws • tempera paints and brushes • tissue paper • transparent tape • washable markers

What About Television?

For me, the key to the whole "children and television" issue is not so much what the children watch, because we can control that if we want to. My main concern about children and television is more about how parents use television in their home, and what children do not do when they watch television. It is easy to use the television as a babysitter on occasion, but it can be habit-forming to both parent and child. The few short years of early childhood can quickly be gobbled up by thousands of hours of TV viewing time that could and should have been spent playing, reading, walking, talking, painting, crafting: time spent together.

But television, for better or worse, is here to stay. As parents we can control it and use it in such a way that it will be beneficial to our child's development and to the parent/child relationship. First of all, be selective in what your children watch. Good television programs can make learning fun and can expand your child's knowledge of the world. Programs like Sesame Street can even help your child get ready for school. On the other hand, many programs on television today are far from innocent or educational and can be very detrimental to our children's emotional, intellectual, and spiritual well-being. So choose wisely; look for programs or videotapes which instruct, entertain, and reinforce the values and principles you wish to develop in your child.

Second, limit your child's viewing time each day. Remember, time spent watching TV is time that your child does not spend on other, more valuable, activities, such as playing games, reading (or being read to), or using his imagination in countless other ways. Children who spend a lot of time watching television can come to expect the instant stimulation that a fast-paced show can bring, and may be less likely to use their own imagination and creativity to stimulate themselves.

Third, when possible, watch television with your child. Most programs move at such a fast pace that children have a hard time keeping track of the content. It is almost impossible for children to stop and ponder what is being presented. Parents can provide connections that the children miss. By reminding your child of related events in his own life, you help him make sense of what he sees.

Finally, set an example for your child. Show him that you would rather read a book or play a game or talk to him than watch TV. It's hard to expect your child to learn to limit his viewing and choose programs wisely when you do just the opposite. Remember, children learn from our actions more than our words.

A Word of Encouragement

Motherhood brings as much joy as ever, but it still brings boredom, exhaustion, and sorrow too. Nothing else will ever make you as happy or as sad, as proud or as tired, for nothing is quite as hard as helping a person develop his own individuality — especially while you struggle to keep your own.

MARGUERITE KELLY AND ELIA PARSONS

Be encouraged as you weather the stormy seas of parenting. Raising a child is a monumental task which brings with it a great amount of work, but you need not (and should not!) spend 100 percent of your time catering to the needs or wants of your preschooler. By providing your child with daily activities that are simple and fun, by placing more importance on your child's happiness and learning than on the appearance of your home, and by talking to your child on a level he understands, you help him become more capable and confident. Not only will he be better prepared for school when the time comes, but, in the process, you help to make many happy memories of childhood.

CHAPTER TWO

Rainy Day Play

The years rush past, as every older woman will tell the young mothers who complain that they still have two little ones at home and it seems like forever before they will all be in school. Oh no, they say — time flies — enjoy them while they're young — they grow up so fast…

The mothers agree that indeed the years do fly. It's the days that don't. The hours, minutes of a single day sometimes just stop. And a mother finds herself standing in the middle of a room wondering. Wondering. Years fly. Of course they do. But a mother can gag on a day.

JAIN SHERRARD

LIFE WITH PRESCHOOLERS CAN BE A WONDERFUL, REWARDING EXPERIENCE. On long, warm, summer days, when adults and children alike can be outside from sunup to sundown, parenting can seem very fun and easy. But "fun" and "easy" are not words you are likely to hear from anyone who has endured a week of rain with several house-bound preschoolers. Most preschoolers have a great amount of energy, but a relatively short attention span. Boredom can cause acutely irritating behaviour in small children, and should be avoided as much as possible. Now is the time for big, messy art projects (see Chapter 8) and marathon baking sessions. Invite friends for lunch frequently, and always be prepared with something fun for the children to do indoors.

The activities which follow are especially suited to indoor play. Some require a table or counter top, and some require water — these are best-suited to your kitchen. Other water-related activities are a natural for the bathroom and bath-time. The rest are more flexible, and can be easily adapted to the bedroom, living room, family room, or other room in the house that has plenty of floor space and an absence of breakables.

CLEAN COINS

> Old toothbrush
> Soap
> Water
> Bowl
> Coins
> Dishcloth or paper towel
> Salt and vinegar (optional)

Your child can practice cleaning coins with an old toothbrush and some soap and water. Fill a bowl with a small amount of water and place a few coins in the bowl. Your child will have fun brushing the coins with soap to make them look brand new. When the coins are as clean as your child can make them, dry them with a dishcloth or paper towel.

For super-shiny coins, mix a small amount of salt and vinegar in a bowl. Drop the coins in and watch the tarnish fade. (If you do use vinegar, make sure your child does not get any in her eyes; soap is bad enough, but vinegar will really sting!)

SUPER SUDS

> Liquid detergent
> Water
> Bowl
> Eggbeater
> Straw (optional)

Put a few drops of liquid detergent into a bowl and fill it halfway with water. Use an eggbeater to whip up some suds in the soapy water, or a big straw to blow some really big bubbles. This also works well at the kitchen sink; fill the sink with soapy water and pull up a chair for your child to stand on as she plays.

As a variation, fill a sink with warm soapy water; give your child spoons, a whisk, and plastic bowls and dishes, and let her have fun with water.

MUSICAL GLASSES

> Drinking glasses
> Water
> Spoon

Fill drinking glasses with different amounts of water and have your child lightly tap the glasses with a spoon. Notice the different sounds each glass makes. Try to play simple tunes, or make up your own melodies as you play.

WASHING WINDOWS

> Spray bottle
> Water
> Vinegar
> Cleaning cloth

Fill a spray bottle with water and a quarter cup white vinegar. Give your child the bottle and cleaning cloth and let her help you wash the windows, bathroom counters, or kitchen appliances. She will love to be your helper and work along side you while you do some of your own cleaning.

BATH BUDDY

> Bar of soap
> Washcloth
> Thread
> Needle
> Small scrap of fabric or felt for eyes
> Scissors

Wrap a washcloth around a bar of soap and sew the open ends together, encasing the soap completely. Cut eye shapes out of fabric or felt, and sew the eyes on top of the washcloth-covered soap. If you like, sew on a mouth, nose, eyebrows, and any other details for more fun. Your child will have fun lathering up in the bath with her new bath buddy.

BATH PAINTS

This is an all-time favourite with our children, but merits a few words of caution. If you have ceramic tile in your bathtub area, you may want to skip this one, as the food colouring may stain the grout. If your child has sensitive skin, the shaving cream (depending on the brand) can cause irritation. In any case, children will almost certainly need another bath when this activity is over!

Shaving cream
Food colouring
Muffin tin
Spoon
Paintbrushes or sponge

Squirt shaving cream into the individual sections of a muffin tin. Add a few drops of food colouring to each section and mix with a spoon. The kids will love painting the walls, the tub and themselves with their hands, a sponge, or paintbrushes. Older children will enjoy mixing the individual colours to create new ones. Clean up is easy—when the fun ends just hose down the tub, with your child in it!

WATER RAINBOW

Eyedropper
Small containers of water
Food colouring

Give your child an eyedropper and several small containers of water coloured with a few drops of food colouring. Let her arrange the colours to create a rainbow, mix colours, or drop water into other empty containers.

COUNT THE COINS

Pennies or other coins

Give your child a jar of pennies or other coins and have her count them and place them in stacks of five or ten. Then count the stacks. Talk to her about what money can and cannot buy by giving her examples: "Can money buy us food?" "...good friends?" "...clothes?" "...a new baby sister?"

INDOOR SANDBOX

> Cardboard box or plastic baby bath
> Puffed wheat or rice cereal
> Sandbox toys

Create an indoor sandbox by filling a cardboard box, plastic baby bath or basin with inexpensive puffed wheat or rice cereal. Use buckets, shovels, and dump trucks, or measuring cups, spoons, and bowls. Clean up is easy! (Uncooked rice can be inexpensive when bought in bulk, and it makes an interesting road surface for small trucks or other wheeled toys.)

PAPER CLIP JEWELRY

> Paper clips

Show your child how to link paper clips together to form a necklace or bracelet. Use standard metal clips or bright plastic ones, or a combination of the two.

PAPER PUNCH

> Hole punch
> Paper scraps

Give your child a hole punch and scraps of paper in various colours. She will amuse herself for quite some time making confetti that can be saved and used for art and craft activities.

WHO LOVES YOU?

> Paper and pen
> Markers and/or stickers for decorating

Ask your child, "Who loves you?" and write down her answer. Ask, "Who else loves you?" and write down each name, then read her the list when she is finished. Top the list with the title, "Look Who Loves (child's name)" and let her decorate it with markers or stickers. Stick it on the refrigerator or on her bedroom wall to remind her how much she is loved.

INDOOR TENT

Sheet or blanket
Empty table

Place a sheet or blanket over a table to make an indoor tent. Put a special snack inside and give your child a flashlight. If you like, furnish the tent with pillows and a blanket, and let your child camp out all morning.

WRITE A STORY

Look in your local library for books or information on making books with children. Stories turned into books will be treasured for years to come.

Paper
Pen, markers or crayons
Photographs or old magazines
Scissors
Glue

Write a story with your child about events in her life, a story in which she is the central character. Begin the story by saying, for example, "Today is a special day for (child's name) because she is going to _____." Write the story down, including your child's responses, and illustrate the story with drawings, photos, or pictures cut from magazines. Your child can help you choose and glue in the pictures.

SHARPEN A PENCIL

This might not hold her attention for long, but you may be surprised!

Pencils or crayons
Pencil or crayon sharpener
Small plate or cup

Your preschooler will no doubt have a lot of fun sharpening pencils. Give her a pencil sharpener, pencil, and a small plate or cup to catch the shavings. For younger children, it is probably better to use crayons and a crayon sharpener. (Save the crayon shavings to use when making Stained Glass Crayons, Rainbow Crayons, or Wax Paper Art.)

NAIL BOARD

Nails
Wood
Hammer
String or elastic bands

Hammer nails into a piece of board and allow your child to create a design by wrapping string or coloured elastic bands around the nails. Hammer the nails in a pattern, or use rows or circles so your child can create her own designs. Make sure that the nails only penetrate the top side of the board, put away the hammer and excess nails, and supervise your child to avoid accidents.

LISTENING GAME

Have your child close her eyes and guess the sounds you make. Use household objects such as keys, coins, silverware, or a whistle. Tap on a pot with a spoon, snap your fingers, or click your tongue.

WHAT'S MISSING?

Various household objects or small toys

Test your preschooler's memory skills by placing a few toys or household objects in front her. Allow her to study them, then have her close her eyes while you remove one object. See if she can tell you which object is missing.

LITTLE CARPENTER

Golf tees
Styrofoam
Toy hammer

Give your child some golf tees, a toy hammer and a piece of Styrofoam. She can hammer the golf tees into the foam in a design, or just hammer for the sake of hammering.

STICKER PLAY

Stickers from magazine and record clubs

Save all the stickers that come in the mail, the ones advertising records or magazines. Separate them along the perforated lines, and let your child stick them onto a plain piece of paper or decorate her artwork.

MAGNET MAGIC

Refrigerator magnets
Heavy paper

Give your child a couple of refrigerator magnets and a heavy piece of paper. Place the paper between the two magnets and show your child how to move the top magnet by moving the bottom magnet. On the top side of the paper draw a road or some other pattern for your child to follow.

LID ART

Plastic lids from 4-litre milk jugs
Glue
Paper plate or piece of cardboard

If you buy your milk or juice in 4-litre plastic jugs, save the small plastic lids. Once you have a collection of different coloured lids, let your child glue them onto a piece of cardboard or a paper plate to create a design. Kids will also have fun sorting lids by colour, lining them up end to end, creating patterns, or using them as play money.

SETTING THE TABLE

Plates
Silverware
Napkins
Glasses

When you aren't using your best china, have your child help you set the table. Have her count the number of people who will be eating, then count out the same number of knives, forks, spoons, plates, napkins, and so on. Show her how to place everything on the table properly. For younger children, you may want to set the plates and other breakables yourself, and have your child help you with silverware and napkins — unless, of course, you are using paper plates!

I LOVE YOU BECAUSE

> Paper and pen
> Crayons or markers

Ask your child, "Why do you love Daddy?" Write down her responses on a sheet of plain or construction paper and have your child decorate it with crayons or markers. Place the love note as a surprise in Dad's lunch the next day. You can vary the questions you ask your child, such as, "What's the funniest thing Daddy ever did?" You can also try this for grandparents or other friends and relatives. Some of the answers you get may be priceless!

PUT AWAY THE SILVERWARE

> Silverware
> Utensil holder

Your child can help you put away the silverware as you remove it from the dishwasher or drainer. Place your utensil holder on the table with the clean utensils next to it. Your child can then sort, count, and put them away.

NEWSPAPER GOLF

> Newspaper
> Tape
> Golf or tennis balls
> Masking tape or paper

Make golf clubs for each player by rolling up several sheets of newspaper and taping them securely. Lay down a sheet of paper or use masking tape to mark several "holes" on the floor or carpet. Use your golf club to try to hit (roll) the ball to the hole. Reward the winner (the first to hit the ball to the hole) with a raisin, chocolate chip, or other small treat.

SEWING PRACTICE

> Heavy cardboard
> Scissors
> Hole punch
> Shoelace or yarn
> Tape (if using yarn)

Cut a shape out of heavy cardboard and punch holes around the edges at regular intervals. Tie a knot in one end of an old shoelace, or knot one end of a piece of yarn and wrap heavy tape around the other end. Let your child sew by weaving the shoelace through the punched holes. This fun activity is great for hand/eye coordination.

SURPRISE PACKAGE

> Common household object
> Shoe box or other small box
> Wrapping paper

Place a common household object inside a shoe box and cover the box with wrapping paper. Give your child three clues that describe the object in the box. Have her guess what it is before opening the package.

HAND PUPPETS

> Washable markers

Using washable markers, draw a face on the palm of your child's hand, or draw small faces on the pads of each finger so that the puppets can "talk" to each other. Draw puppets on your own fingers and get some conversations going between your puppets and your child's.

FUN WITH WEIGHTS

> Bathroom scale
> Various household objects

Using a bathroom scale, weigh your child and help her to weigh different household objects: a stack of books, bag of flour, dolls, and so on. Try to find something that weighs the same as your child.

SHAPE SHAKE

 Cardboard
 Scissors
 String

Cut out a cardboard shape and pierce a small hole in the centre. Tie one end of a string to the doorknob of your child's room and thread the opposite end of the string through the shape's hole. Have your child stand across the room holding and shaking the free end of the string. See how long it takes her to shake the shape from one end to the other.

FISHING

 Construction paper
 Scissors
 Pen, crayon, or marker
 Small box, pot, or other container

Cut fish shapes out of coloured construction paper. On each fish write a different instruction: "Find something red"; "Count to ten"; "Touch your toes"; and so on. Place the fish in a small box or container and let your child pick one fish at a time. Read the instruction and have her perform it.

LIVING ROOM PICNIC

 Tablecloth and picnic dishes
 Picnic food
 Summer clothing

Brighten the coldest, rainiest, or stormiest of days by having an indoor picnic. Spread a tablecloth on the floor of your living room and use outdoor dishes or paper plates. Picnic-type dress (shorts or bathing suits) is essential, and don't forget your sunglasses.

RED LIGHT/GREEN LIGHT

Stand 20 to 25 feet away from your child. When you say "green light", have her walk, run, hop, skip, or crawl toward you. She must stop when you say "red light".

MEMORY

Index cards
Pen or marker
Stickers (optional)

Sharpen your preschooler's memory skills by making your own memory game. Create two identical sets of index cards with letters of the alphabet, colours, shapes, or numbers, or use two sets of stickers to make a picture version of this game. Start out with only a few, as this can be tough. Place all the cards, face down, on the table. Have your child turn over one card, then try to find the corresponding matching card. If she picks the matching card within a predetermined number of tries, she takes the pair. If she doesn't get a match, the first card gets turned face down again and she has to start again. You can make a game out of this between two or more children to see who can collect the most pairs. At first your child may only guess, but it won't take long for her to get the idea. Begin the game with only a few cards, and add more as your child gets better; don't overwhelm her with too many cards at once.

SORT THE LAUNDRY

Laundry

This is a great activity that will give your child some household responsibility and teach a very practical skill at the same time. Show your child how to sort the laundry before you wash it. Even a very young child can separate whites, colours, and darks, and it will save you time as well! You can also have your child remove the clothes from the dryer, and sort and carry them to the appropriate rooms when folded. Folding may be a little tricky depending on your standards, but you can let her tackle the easy things: towels, dish cloths, baby blankets, and so on.

SORTING SOCKS

Socks
Laundry basket

Take all the socks out of your child's sock drawer. Have her identify each colour as she puts them back in. For some real fun, give your child a laundry basket and have her collect all the socks from every sock drawer in the house. She can amuse herself for a long time by sorting them by colour, size, or owner. If you like, separate the socks, mix them all up, and then have your child find the matches for each sock. Keep in mind, however, that you may have to rematch most of the socks yourself after your child is done.

Sock Toss

> Soft ball or rolled up socks
> Empty laundry basket

Using rolled up socks or a small soft ball, place an empty laundry basket on the floor and have your child toss the ball or socks into the basket from several feet away. Place the basket on top of a table or dresser for a game of indoor basketball.

CARPET RACEWAY

> Books or scraps of wood
> Matchbox cars or other toys with wheels

Make a raceway or train track on a carpet by laying down books of equal thickness side by side to make a smooth lane, or use pieces of plywood or two-by-fours. (Your raceway can be any length and can be straight or have turns.) This will transform the carpet into a smooth surface for racing toys with wheels.

DoLL CLoSET

> Tension rod
> Baby clothes hangers
> Bookcase

Make a closet for all those little doll clothes by inserting a tension rod across the lower shelf of a bookcase. Have your child hang doll clothes onto baby clothes hangers and then onto the rod. (Try to save some of your newborn-sized clothes, bibs, and blankets; they are the perfect size for many dolls.)

HOTTER/COLDER

Small toys or edible treats

Hide several household objects, small toys or edible treats around the house and encourage your child to find them. Tell her she is "hotter" when she is closer to the hidden item, "colder" as she moves away from it.

INDOOR CAMPING

Sleeping bags
Marshmallows

Don't let the weather stop you – to a preschooler, indoor camping can be just as fun. Lay out the sleeping bags in front of the fireplace, if you have one. Eat marshmallows, or make S'Mores (see Chapter 3) in the microwave, and sing campfire songs. Strum on a guitar if you can, and turn the night into a precious memory for you and your child.

PILLOW THROW

If you have any breakables on tables or dressers, you might want to put them away before trying this one!

Lots of throw pillows

Have one person sit on a bed or couch with the throw pillows. The other person runs across the room from one point to another, while the person on the bed tries to hit the moving target with the pillows.

TELL ME A STORY

Various household objects
Pillowcase or brown paper bag

Put five or six various household objects into a brown paper bag or pillow case: keys, purse, stuffed animal, book, and so on. Remove each item from the bag one at a time, and create a story by adding one sentence for each item as it is removed: "Once upon a time there was a little monkey named George. George just loved to read books, especially books about cars."

NIGHT AT THE MOVIES

Family video or favourite movie
Special snack

Whether your child watches a little television or a lot, you can still make an occasion out of watching a special program or movie together. Snuggle under a blanket or lie on the floor. Dim the lights and have a special snack together.

HIDE AND SEEK

Kitchen timer

Wind up your kitchen timer and hide it somewhere in the house. Have your child search for it by listening for its ticking sound.

BALANCING BOARD

Board measuring about 8 inches wide by 6 feet long
Magazines or other books

Place the board across two piles of magazines. Have your child practice keeping her balance by walking across the board. As your child grows more steady, you can place one end on a chair and she can walk up it, or across two chairs as she grows even more bold. Remember, though: The higher you build the balance beam, the more supervision your child will need.

SHOE TRAIL

Empty laundry basket
Shoes

Give your child a laundry basket and have her fill it with shoes. Make a trail of shoes around the house, lining them up heel to toe. Follow the trail, counting as you go. Keep a list, and have your child count how many shoes each person has, or how many shoes of each colour there are, or how many shoes there are in total. Help your child put the shoes away when she is done.

BEAN BAG TOSS

The zippered freezer bag protects the beans even if the bag gets wet.

> Zippered freezer bag
> Dried beans
> 4-by-6-inch scraps of material
> Needle and thread

Make a homemade bean bag by filling a small zippered freezer bag with dried beans. Sew together two squares of material with right sides facing in, leaving a space on the fourth side big enough to slide in the bag of beans. Turn the bag right side out, insert the bag of beans, then sew up the space. (If you don't have time to sew a bean bag, pour beans into an old sock, knot the open end, and turn down the cuff.) Use the bean bag to play catch, or have your child toss the bag into an empty laundry basket from a few feet away.

CHAIR MAZE

> Chairs

This activity will work well outdoors or in. Place chairs in a maze around the room. Let your child crawl through them or walk over them, or use them as a train for her stuffed animals.

GO FISH

> Stick for fishing pole
> String
> Magnet
> Scissors
> Construction paper
> Glue or tape
> Metal paper clips

Cut fish shapes out of construction paper. Glue or tape metal paper clips to the back of each fish. Make a fishing pole out of a long stick and a length of string. Tie a magnet on the end of the string. Go fishing. This works well if you place the "fish" on the floor and let your child dangle her line over the back of the couch. You can also use this game to help your child learn her basic skills: Draw a shape or write a letter or number on the back of each fish, and have her identify it when caught.

ANIMAL CHARADES

Variety of stuffed animals
Pillowcase

Place several stuffed animals in a pillowcase. Close your eyes while your child takes one out and looks at it. Have her put it back in the case and act out the animal while you try to guess what it is.

FOLLOW THE LEADER

Have your child follow you through the house, imitating the sounds and movements you make. You can dance around, pretend to be a bunny or a horse, a train or a car, and so on. Take turns and let your child lead you.

MAKE A TAPE

Tape recorder
Blank cassette tape

If you have access to a tape recorder, help your child make a tape for Dad to play on his way to work. Sing favourite songs, say nursery rhymes, tell him a story, talk about what you do when he's at work, tell him you love him and why you're thankful for him. This makes a great Father's Day gift. You can also use this idea for a grandparent or other special person.

PLAY WITH BOXES

Cardboard boxes in various sizes

Your child can put supermarket boxes of all sizes to good use. She can have a train for herself or her animals, build a fort, make a dollhouse, or ride in a car. You can be sure she will think of something new every time she plays with these boxes.

INDOOR TREASURE HUNT

> Small toys or snacks
> Treasure map (optional)

This is a great way to liven up a rainy day. Have an indoor treasure hunt by hiding several small toys, books, or special snacks around the house. Give your child clues or draw a map that leads to the treasure.

TIMER FUN

Although you can easily buy a timer, I like the idea of making one instead. Older preschoolers will enjoy measuring the sand and timing it as it flows from top to bottom. Children of all ages will enjoy using the timer for some fun one-minute games.

> Two baby food jars or other small jars with lids
> Hammer
> Nail
> Sand or salt
> Glue gun
> Coloured tape or ribbon (optional)

Use a hammer and nail to make a hole in the centre of each jar lid. Fill one of the jars with sand, then screw on the lid. Place the other jar, with its lid on, directly over the first jar. Carefully flip the jars over so that the jar with sand in it is now on top of the empty jar. Using a clock with a second hand, a digital watch, or a timer, see how much sand will go from the top jar to the bottom jar in one minute. Quickly remove the top jar and throw away any leftover sand before replacing the lid on the jar. (If you ran out of sand before the minute was up, put more sand in and time it again.) Carefully put hot glue over the top of the jar with sand in it, then place the empty jar back on top of the full one. Secure the lids together with coloured tape or ribbon if you like.

You now have a sturdy one-minute timer. You can use this to play a variety of games, such as a matching game ("How many cards can you match in one minute?"), a pick-up game ("How many blocks can you put in the basket in one minute?"), or a movement game ("How many jumps can you make in one minute?"). Be creative in coming up with other uses for your timer.

SIMON SAYS

This old favourite is a fun game to play with your child. Have your child follow your actions only when you say "Simon says": "Simon says touch your toes"; "Simon says stretch your arms"; "Simon says jump up and down." Your child should remain motionless when you give a command that is not preceded by "Simon says." This is a lot of fun when done very quickly, and is a good game for a group. You can have each child sit down if she moves when she's not supposed to, and award a small prize to the last child who remains standing. Take turns being Simon.

WHOSE EAR IS THIS?

> Blindfold

For this activity you will need at least three people. Take turns blindfolding each other and try to guess who each person is just by touching one feature: nose, finger, ear, hair, and so on.

PRETEND ISLANDS

> Pillows

Place pillows on the carpet for pretend islands, and imagine the carpet is the ocean. Have your child jump from island to island without falling in the water.

CHAPTER THREE

Kids in the Kitchen

You cannot teach a child to take care of himself unless you let him try to take care of himself. He will make mistakes; and out of these mistakes will come his wisdom.

FRANCIS BACON

W ORK AND PLAY ARE INSEPARABLE FOR KIDS; YOUR WORK IS VERY OFTEN your child's play. The kitchen is a wonderful place for children, and whether you are in there a little or a lot, your child will naturally want to be with you when you are.

Full of many irresistible things to see, touch, taste and smell, the kitchen can also be a hazardous place for unsupervised children. Remember to always be safety-conscious. Make sure any dangerous objects are well out of reach, and be sure to closely supervise any use of sharp utensils, the oven or the stove. Better yet, make a rule that only an adult can use those things.

The kitchen can be a tremendously stimulating environment for young children, so try to provide a different kitchen activity as often as possible. Consider providing your child with his very own Baker's Box (see Chapter 1), and don't forget the non-food activities for the kitchen in Chapter 2. Getting dinner on the table at the "arsenic hour" will be less of an ordeal if you make special plans to keep your child busy.

Fun With Food

Anyone who has ever watched a small child eat will know that as much as food is meant to be eaten, to a child it is also something to be played with. Children, even as young as two, will enjoy making their own peanut butter sandwiches, and most will agree that finger Jell-O is one of the best foods ever invented! Make sure your child's hands are clean, accept that things may get a little messy, and let your child enjoy his food experience.

FRUIT KEBABS

> Small wooden skewers, Popsicle sticks, coffee stirrers or swizzle
>   sticks
> Various fruit, cut into bite-sized pieces

Have your child create fruit kebabs by putting pieces of fruit onto small wooden skewers, wooden Popsicle sticks, plastic coffee stirrers, or swizzle sticks. As your child works, talk to him about the different types of fruit, their colours, smells and tastes. Serve the kebabs for dessert or a tasty snack.

TASTE TESTING

> Blindfold
> Various food items

Blindfold your child and have him identify by taste and smell some of his favourite foods (ice cream, pickles, yogurt, cereal, cookies, and so on). Have him describe the different tastes and textures and ask him to group them as sweet, salty, bitter, sour, spicy, or tangy.

MELON BOWL

> Watermelon
> Other melons (honeydew, cantaloupe)
> Knife
> Melon-ball scoop

Make a watermelon bowl by cutting a watermelon in half. Have your child scoop out the melon with a melon-ball scoop. Cut open several other melons and have him continue to make more melon balls. Fill the watermelon bowl with the melon balls and serve as a summer dessert or tasty afternoon snack.

HAPPY-FACE SANDWICH

    Bread
    Peanut butter
    Raisins or chocolate chips
    Knife

Spread peanut butter on one side of a piece of bread. Have your child decorate it with eyes, a nose, and a big, happy smile made of raisins or chocolate chips.

MINI-POPSICLES

    Empty ice cube tray
    Juice
    Fruit (grapes, raisins, cherries)
    Toothpicks

Fill an empty ice cube tray with juice, and put one or two pieces of fruit (grapes, raisins, and cherries work well) and one toothpick inside each compartment. Freeze and enjoy.

FLOUR DRAWING

    Cookie sheet
    Flour

Lightly sprinkle the surface of a cookie sheet with flour. Show your child how to draw in it with his finger. Or draw a letter, number or shape in the flour with your finger and have him draw the same next to yours.

PUDDING PAINTS

    Packaged pudding mix

Prepare packaged pudding mix ahead of time, and when cooled allow your child to fingerpaint on a plastic or paper plate, tabletop, or other smooth surface. This may not be suitable before a meal, but there probably won't be much left to clean up!

HoMEMADE PEANUT BUTTER

Shelling enough peanuts to make a little peanut butter is sure to keep your child busy.

Peanuts in the shell
Food processor
Small container or baby food jar (optional)
Decorative fabric and ribbon (optional)

Place the shelled peanuts in your food processor and grind until smooth. Store in a covered container. To give as a gift, place the peanut butter in a small baby food jar with lid. Cover the lid with a circle of fabric, and tie a ribbon around the neck of the jar to keep the fabric in place.

PASTA PLAY

Dried pasta
Bowls
Measuring cups
Mixing spoons

Give your child containers filled with various sizes and shapes of dried pasta, such as macaroni, rotini, shells, and so on. Add a few empty bowls, measuring cups, and a mixing spoon or two, and let your child measure, mix, and match. If you like, give your child string and let him make necklaces, bracelets, ornaments, and other objects. (Supervise young children to avoid strangulation.) As an option, dye the pasta using the directions for pasta dye in Appendix A, Basic Craft Recipes. For a variation, try using cereal, dried beans, or rice in place of pasta.

CHASE THE PEPPER

Your child will love to show off this neat trick.

Pie plate or small sink
Pepper
Bar of soap
Sugar

Fill a pie plate or small sink with water. Shake pepper on the water and dip a piece of wet soap into it. The pepper will run away from the soap. Now shake some sugar into the clear area and the pepper will run back.

S'MORES

You don't need to go camping to enjoy these yummy treats.

> Graham wafers
> Piece of chocolate (or use chocolate chips)
> Marshmallows

Place a graham wafer on a microwaveable plate or piece of paper towel. Top with a piece of chocolate (or several chocolate chips) and a marshmallow. Microwave on high for 20 seconds or until the marshmallow starts to puff up. Remove from the microwave, top with another graham wafer, and enjoy!

APPLE SHAPES

> Apples
> Metal cookie cutters
> Knife

Peel apples and cut them into thin slices. Give your child small metal cookie cutters and let him cut shapes out of the slices.

BANANA BALLS

> Ripe bananas
> Bowl
> Fork
> Finely chopped nuts
> Cinnamon
> Cookie sheet

Have your child mash a ripe banana in a bowl with a fork. Add finely chopped nuts and a dash of cinnamon, and mix. Form the mixture into small balls and place the balls on a cookie sheet. When all the balls are complete, cover the cookie sheet and refrigerate. These are great for a quick snack or for floating in cereal and milk for breakfast.

Cooking With Kids

The kitchen is a tantalizing place for children, full of wonderful things to smell, touch and taste. With a little bit of effort and a lot of patience on your part, it can also become a wonderful classroom for your child. Talk to him about the magic of the kitchen, how yeast or baking powder makes things rise, how the batter baked in the oven turns into a cake, how cornstarch thickens a sauce. He will want to help you measure and mix, wash vegetables, cut out cookies, and sift dry ingredients. Include him in your work and take the time to teach him as you go. Make or buy your child his own recipe box and copy out his favourite recipes, using simple words, pictures and symbols. Include some simple "no-cook" recipes that he can make with little supervision.

"But is it really worth all the trouble?," the tired Mom will ask. "Isn't it easier just to do it myself?" Sure it is. In my own experience there were many times when I would rather have had no little hands "helping" me. But I now have two daughters who can bake delicious cookies, muffins and squares among other things. Andria, at barely nine years old, once made tea, toast, and scrambled eggs for the entire family while looking after the baby and allowing me an extra hour of sleep. At four, my son's favourite thing to do was bake bread with me. Now, with all the nostalgia of a seven-year-old, he reminisces about those fun mornings we had together, and he still enjoys working with me in the kitchen.

ANIMAL PANCAKES

 1¼ cups all-purpose flour
 2 Tbsp. sugar
 2 tsp. baking powder
 ¾ tsp. salt
 3 Tbsp. salad oil
 1⅓ cups milk
 1 egg, slightly beaten

In a large bowl, with fork, mix the flour, sugar, baking powder and salt. Add the salad oil, milk and egg and stir just until the flour mixture is moistened. Preheat an electric griddle or skillet; grease lightly with salad oil. Use a spoon to drop the batter into the pan to make animal shapes. A bunny needs only a round shape for the head and two long shapes for ears (and maybe chocolate chips or blueberries for eyes). Try to make a mouse with an oval body, smaller drops for the head, ears and feet, and a long thin tail. A turtle can be one big spoonful of batter surrounded by six smaller drops. Try a cat, bird, giraffe, elephant – use your imagination!

AGGRESSION COOKIES

This is truly one recipe your child can make all by himself. You may need to help him measure the ingredients, but the mixing he won't need any help with!

 3 cups quick-cooking oats
 1½ cups brown sugar
 1½ cups flour
 1½ cups butter or margarine
 1½ tsp. baking powder

Dump all the ingredients into a large bowl and let your child really go at it! Pound, punch, and knead the batter – the longer and harder the dough is mixed, the better the cookies will taste! When ready to bake, preheat the oven to 350 degrees. Roll the dough into small balls and bake on ungreased cookie sheets for 10 to 12 minutes.

Snow-Topped Cupcakes

1 egg
1 cup milk
1 tsp. vanilla
1¼ cup white sugar
½ cup margarine, melted
1¾ cup flour
2½ tsp. baking powder
½ tsp. salt
White frosting
Shredded coconut

Preheat the oven to 350 degrees. Combine the egg, milk, vanilla, sugar and margarine in a large bowl and blend on medium speed with electric mixer. Add flour, baking powder and salt, and mix on the top speed of mixer for 2 minutes. Pour into paper-lined muffin tins. Bake for 20 minutes. Let your child frost the cupcakes with white frosting and dip them in coconut for snow. Serve them for dinner or a teddy-bear tea.

Alphabet Cookies

This special vanilla dough handles like modelling clay, but also makes delicious cookies. Use this activity to strengthen your child's alphabet skills. The finished products make good place cards for children's birthday parties.

4½ cups unsifted all-purpose flour
1½ cups butter
3 hard-cooked egg yolks
¾ cup sugar
3 raw egg yolks
1½ tsp. vanilla

Measure flour into a large bowl. Cut butter into small pieces and add to the flour. Mix with your fingers until the flour and butter form fine crumbs. Mash cooked egg yolks with sugar and stir into the flour mixture. Blend raw egg yolks with vanilla and stir into the flour mixture with a fork. Press the mixture with your hands into a firm ball. Work with the dough at room temperature, but cover and refrigerate it if you plan to shape and bake it later. Preheat the oven to 300 degrees.

Roll out the dough. Cut 3-inch or 4-inch strips and roll with your palm to make ropes. Shape the ropes into letters. Flatten them slightly so they are about ¼-inch thick. If you like, decorate the letters with coloured sugar or chocolate chips. Place the letters on a cookie sheet and bake for 25 to 30 minutes.

PAINTBOX COOKIES

These sturdy cookies, baked and glazed ahead, can be painted with food colouring for a rainy day or party project.

> 2 cups softened butter or margarine
> 2 cups granulated sugar
> 2 tsp. vanilla
> 5 cups flour
> 5-9 tsp. warm water
> 1½ lb. icing sugar
> Food colouring

Preheat oven to 300 degrees. Beat butter, granulated sugar and vanilla together. Add flour and mix until thoroughly blended. Roll out the dough on an ungreased baking sheet to ¼ to ⅜ inch thickness. Cut into shapes with a knife or floured cookie cutters. Bake for 25 to 30 minutes until dough is a pale golden colour. Let cookies cool on pan about 7 minutes, then transfer to foil-covered surface.

To make icing, add warm water to icing sugar until icing is smooth and thick. Spread the icing onto the cookies, making a smooth surface. Let the icing dry thoroughly (8 to 24 hours) before covering or moving the cookies.

When the icing is dry, paint on it with food colouring. Use a paintbrush and small cups of food colouring undiluted for bright colours or slightly diluted for lighter ones. Food colouring will flow, so allow each colour to dry briefly before adding the next.

Note: If making the cookies ahead of time, complete the steps up to and including the icing stage, and then store the cookies at room temperature for up to four days. Freeze for longer storage. Thaw before painting.

CHOCOLATE PIZZA PIE

 1 cup + ¾ cup semi-sweet chocolate chips
 ½ cup + 2 Tbsp. golden flavour shortening
 ½ cup all-purpose flour
 ½ cup granulated sugar
 2 eggs
 1 tsp. baking powder
 2 Tbsp. water
 Assorted candy for decoration

Preheat the oven to 350 degrees. Melt 1 cup chocolate chips and ½ cup shortening in a double boiler; cool. Add flour, sugar, eggs, and baking powder; mix well. Spread evenly onto well greased 12-inch pizza pan. Bake for 15 minutes. Cool. Combine ¾ cup chocolate chips, 2 Tbsp. shortening, and 2 Tbsp. water in a double boiler. Melt and stir to combine. Spread glaze evenly over cooled chocolate pizza. Decorate with candies.

BEST CHOCOLATE CHIP COOKIES IN THE WORLD

These cookies are great! Be sure to refrigerate the dough before baking, and don't overbake them; they harden as they cool. Double the batch and freeze half of the dough for instant, no-mess baking fun on a rainy day.

 ½ cup margarine, room temperature
 ½ cup unsalted butter, room temperature
 1 cup packed dark brown sugar
 1 cup granulated sugar
 2 eggs, lightly beaten
 2 Tbsp. milk
 2 tsp. vanilla extract
 2 cups sifted all-purpose flour
 1 tsp. baking powder
 1 tsp. baking soda
 1 tsp. salt
 2 cups quick-cooking oats
 1 cup (or more) chocolate chips
 1 cup coarsely chopped walnuts

Cream the margarine, butter, and both sugars in a large bowl until light and fluffy. Add the eggs, milk, and vanilla and beat until blended. Sift the flour, baking powder, baking soda, and salt together and add to the butter mixture. Stir just until blended. Stir in the oats. Fold in the chocolate chips and walnuts. Cover the dough and refrigerate for at least one hour.

Preheat the oven to 350 degrees. Grease the cookie sheets. Shape the dough into balls, using a rounded teaspoon for small cookies or a scant tablespoon for large. Flatten slightly into rounded disks. Place 2 inches apart on the cookie sheet. Bake until the edges are slightly browned but the cookies are still white, 8 to 10 minutes. Remove from the oven and let cool for 5 minutes. Transfer to wire racks to cool completely.

PEANUT BUTTER oAT SQUARES

These are delicious for adults and children alike!

½ cup butter, softened
1 cup brown sugar, lightly packed
½ cup corn syrup
1 tsp. salt
2 tsp. vanilla
4 cups quick-cooking oats
½ cup peanut butter
½ cup chocolate chips
1½ tsp. butter

Preheat the oven to 350 degrees. Cream the butter and brown sugar in a mixing bowl. Add corn syrup, salt, vanilla and oats. Mix well. Spread mixture evenly in a greased 9-by-13 inch baking pan. Bake for 15 minutes. Cool slightly. Spread peanut butter evenly over top. Combine chocolate chips and butter together in a small saucepan and melt until smooth. Drizzle over peanut butter, or dot onto the peanut butter with a small spoon and use the point of a knife to swirl the chocolate around. Cool until the chocolate sets, then cut into squares.

FANTASTIC FUDGE BROWNIES

Everyone loves a brownie! This is a great rainy day project and something a friend or neighbour will really appreciate.

Batter:

1 cup butter
2 cups sugar
4 heaping Tbsp. cocoa
4 eggs, beaten
1 cup flour
1 cup walnuts, chopped
1 tsp. vanilla

Icing:

2 cups icing sugar
2 Tbsp. butter
2 Tbsp. cocoa
2 Tbsp. boiling water
2 tsp. vanilla

Preheat the oven to 350 degrees. Grease a 9-by-13-inch baking pan. Cream sugar, cocoa, and butter in a large bowl. Add beaten eggs and vanilla. Then add flour and fold in walnuts. Spread batter in the greased baking pan and bake for 30 minutes. The top will appear to be underdone (falls in the middle), but don't overcook. These brownies should be moist and chewy.

While the brownies are baking, mix all the icing ingredients together in a medium bowl with an electric mixer. Ice the brownies immediately after removing from oven so the icing will melt into a shiny glaze.

COOKIE CUT-OUTS

This is the tastiest rolled cookie recipe I've found.

2½ cups flour
1 tsp. cinnamon
½ tsp ginger (optional)
½ tsp. baking powder
¼ tsp. baking soda

¼ tsp. salt
¾ cup butter
½ cup liquid honey
⅓ cup granulated sugar
1 egg

Stir together flour, cinnamon, ginger, baking powder, baking soda, and salt in a medium bowl. Set aside. In a large bowl, cream together butter, honey, and sugar until smooth. Beat in egg. Stir in flour mixture, mixing well. Cover and refrigerate dough for 1½ hours or until firm enough to roll and cut. Preheat the oven to 350 degrees.

Roll out the firm dough on well-floured surface, about one-third of the dough at a time. Cut into desired shapes using floured cutters. Place on a lightly greased cookie sheet. Bake for 8 to 10 minutes until lightly browned and firm to touch. Makes 3 to 4 dozen cookies.

Note: You can decorate these with coloured sugar or sprinkles before baking, or, when cool, cover with icing and then decorate.

PEANUT BUTTER CUPS

This is a very easy and tasty recipe that kids can make themselves with a little help.

2 cups chocolate or carob chips
2 cups peanut butter
3 cups Rice Krispies

Roll the rice cereal between wax paper until it is a powdery texture. Melt the chocolate or carob chips in a double boiler; remove from heat. Add the peanut butter and cereal powder. Mix well. Divide the mixture evenly among the muffin cups, smooth the surface, and cool in the refrigerator to harden.

You may want to line the muffin cups with aluminum foil, or spray them with vegetable spray so the cups will come out easier. Paper muffin liners are not recommended, as the paper will absorb the oil from the peanut butter.

POPCORN BALL CREATURES

¾ cup sugar
1 tsp. white vinegar
I cup brown sugar
½ cup light corn syrup
½ cup water
¼ tsp. salt
¾ cup butter
8 cups popped popcorn

Stir all ingredients except popcorn and butter in a pan over medium heat until the mixture reaches 260 degrees on a candy thermometer (hard ball stage). Reduce temperature to low; add butter. Put popcorn in a large bowl. Pour the mixture over it until the popcorn is coated. Cool slightly. Butter your child's hands and let him mould the popcorn into animal shapes. Place shapes on wax paper until ready to eat.

CRUNCH AND MUNCH

This is a wonderful snack to munch on as you watch your favourite movie, television show or home video together. But be warned – it's addictive!

½ cup butter or margarine, melted
½ cup honey
1 cup peanuts or other nuts, chopped
12 cups popped popcorn

Preheat the oven to 350 degrees. Combine melted butter or margarine and honey in a small saucepan; heat until well-blended. Add chopped nuts. Pour over the popcorn and mix well. Spread the popcorn mixture in a thin layer on a cookie sheet and bake for 12 minutes, until crisp. Stir often to avoid burning.

RICE KRISPIE POPS

A new way to serve an old favourite!

¼ cup margarine or butter
4 cups miniature or 40 regular marshmallows

5 cups Rice Krispies
Wooden popsicle sticks

Melt margarine in a large saucepan, then add marshmallows and cook over low heat, stirring constantly, until syrupy. Remove from heat, add cereal, and stir until well coated. Shape the mixture into an oval around a wooden popsicle stick.

To make Rice Krispie Tarts: Prepare recipe as above. Add cereal and stir until well coated. Press into a buttered muffin tin to form a tart shell; fill with fresh fruit or ice cream.

PoPSiCLES

1 pkg. Kool-Aid
1 pkg. Jell-O
1¼ cups sugar
¾ cup hot water
¾ cup cold water

Mix the dry ingredients thoroughly in a bowl. Measure 6 Tbsp. of the dry ingredients into another mixing bowl; add the hot and cold water. Pour into Popsicle moulds and freeze. Store the remaining dry ingredients in an airtight container for future use.

LoLLiPoPS

¼ cup butter
¾ cup sugar
½ cup light corn syrup
Food colouring

Evenly space 16 Popsicle sticks on a buttered cookie sheet. In a saucepan, heat butter, sugar, and corn syrup over medium-high heat; stir until it boils. Reduce heat to medium. Cook until mixture reaches 270 degrees on a candy thermometer, stirring often. Add food colouring. Drop the mixture by tablespoon onto the end of each Popsicle stick. Cool. When the lollipops are cool, take them off the cookie sheet and wrap them in plastic wrap.

FINGER JELL-O

The following Finger Jell-O recipes make use of different ingredients, but give basically the same result. Use the recipe that best suits the ingredients you have on hand or prefer to use.

Gelatine / Jell-O Recipe

This recipe uses a combination of unflavoured gelatine and commercial Jell-O.

>   2 envelopes unflavoured gelatine
>   6 oz. package Jell-O
>   2½ cups water

Dissolve unflavoured gelatine in a small bowl or measuring cup with one cup cold water. Set aside. In a medium saucepan, bring 1 cup of water to a boil and add Jell-O. Bring to a boil again and remove from heat. Add gelatine mixture. Stir and add ½ cup cold water. Pour into a lightly greased pan and set in the refrigerator until solid (2 hours). Use cookie cutters or a sharp knife to cut into shapes.

Gelatine / Juice Recipe

Avoid using commercial Jell-O by trying this recipe instead.

>   3 envelopes unflavoured gelatine
>   1 – 12 oz. can frozen juice concentrate
>   12 oz. water

Soften gelatine in the thawed juice concentrate. Bring the water to a boil in a medium saucepan. Add the juice/gelatine mixture to the boiling water and stir until gelatine is dissolved. Add sugar for extra sweetening, if desired. Pour into a lightly greased pan and set in the refrigerator until solid (2 hours). Use cookie cutters or a sharp knife to cut into shapes.

Jell-O Only Recipe

This recipe does not require unflavoured gelatine.

>   2-6-oz. packages Jell-O

2½ cups water

Dissolve Jell-O in 2½ cups boiling water in a medium saucepan. Pour into a lightly greased baking pan and set in the refrigerator until solid (about 3 hours). Use cookie cutters or a sharp knife to cut into shapes.

CHAPTER FOUR
outdoor Adventures

*Any adult who spends even fifteen minutes with a child outdoors finds himself
drawn back to his own childhood, like Alice falling down the rabbit hole.*

SHARON MACLATCHIE

CHILDREN OF ALL AGES HAVE SUCH AN ENDLESS AMOUNT OF ENERGY.
Outdoor play every day, in almost any weather, is essential. Most children
are as happy all bundled up for the snow as they are in shorts in the
summertime. Rain provides countless opportunities for play, whether
walking beneath an umbrella or stomping in the puddles, and a brisk
walk is appropriate almost anytime. Playing outdoors in all types of
weather is great fun for kids. You should encourage your child's outdoor
play every day, and join her whenever you can.

The following suggestions will provide your preschooler with some
fun and interesting things to do outdoors. Most activities require a minimum
of materials, and you will find that by making slight adaptations,
most are suitable for any season and any weather.

KICKBALL

All the balls you can find

Gather together all the balls you can find in your house: tennis balls, soccer
balls, basketballs, beach balls, and so on. Line them up one foot apart
and have your child kick each one. See which one is the easiest to kick,
which one goes the farthest, which one goes the highest, and so on.

SIDEWALK DRAWING

Chalk

Have your child use white or coloured chalk to draw on the sidewalk. Teach her how to play games, such as tic-tac-toe or hangman, or simply let her create masterpieces to her heart's content. The "paper" will always be big enough for whatever project she undertakes, and you won't have to worry about display or storage space when she is done! Special sidewalk chalk is available, but regular chalk will – do just be sure to have lots, as it wears down pretty quickly. Also make sure to limit your child's creativity to your residence's sidewalk, unless you ask the neighbours' permission first.

PAINT THE HOUSE

Paintbrush
Bucket of water
Painter's cap

Give your child a clean paintbrush, a bucket full of water and a painter's cap and let her paint the outside of the house, the car, or the sidewalk. Not only will your child feel proud of doing grown-up stuff, she will actually do something useful in the process, and get fresh air and exercise in addition. If your child is old enough to think that painting with water is silly, put some soap into the water and tell her she is washing the house.

SANDPAPER PLAY

Sandpaper
Wood scraps
Glue (optional)
Paint or markers (optional)

Give your child a piece of sandpaper and some small wood scraps. Show her how to sand the wood, and talk about the difference between rough and well-sanded textures. Sanded scraps of wood can be glued together to create wood sculptures and painted or decorated with markers. To avoid splinters, you may want your child to wear gloves for this activity.

BUBBLE SOLUTION

    2 cups warm water
    1 cup liquid dishwashing soap
    ¼ cup glycerine
    1 tsp. sugar
    Funnel, straws, six-pack plastic beverage holders, or other unbreak-
        able household objects

Mix together water, dishwashing soap, glycerine and sugar. Use various unbreakable objects found around the house to blow spectacular bubbles: funnels, straws, six-pack beverage holders. Dip the objects in the bubble solution and blow through them, or wave them through the air like wands. Store solution in a plastic container with a tight-fitting lid.

BACKYARD CAMPING

    Tent
    Sleeping bags
    Pillows
    Flashlight
    Snack

You don't have to go far to give your preschooler the outdoor experience. On a fine summer night, set up your tent in the backyard. Go for a walk in the dark. If a backyard bonfire is not allowed in your neighbourhood, have a snack and sing-along by the light of a flashlight before you pile into your sleeping bags for the night.

OBSTACLE COURSE

    Miscellaneous outdoor objects

Use a variety of outdoor objects to create an obstacle course your child can run around. Have her run around one way, then have her do the course in reverse. You can time her, or she can race with siblings and friends. Do not use objects that have sharp corners or that can tip over easily. If necessary, cushion objects with pillows and blankets.

BACKYARD PICNIC

Blanket
Picnic food
Outdoor toys

You don't have to trek to the park to have a picnic. Set up a picnic in your own backyard: Spread out a blanket, set up the goodies, and bring out the balls and other outdoor toys to complete the fun. In warmer weather, turn on the sprinkler or fill the kiddy pool for some water play.

HOPSCOTCH

Hopscotch grid
Marker

Hopscotch is a good game for counting, coordination, balance, and improving physical agility (and it's a lot of fun, too). Look for a hopscotch grid at the local schoolyard or draw one on your sidewalk with chalk. Give your child a marker (a small chain works well as a marker), and show her how to throw it onto each consecutively numbered square. Hop on one foot to the end of the grid and back again, being careful not to hop in the square where the marker lays.

WALK IN THE DARK

Flashlight
Wagon or stroller (optional)

For children, there is something almost magical about walking in the dark. Go for a walk in the dark with your child. Bring flashlights with you, and a stroller or wagon for younger children.

WATCH THE SUNSET

Blanket
Snack

On a warm summer night, take a blanket and a special snack and go to a place where you can watch the sunset. You may want to bring crayons or coloured pencils and a pad of paper and have your child try to capture the colours of the sunset in a drawing. If your child is too young to draw a sunset, have her find coloured pencils or crayons to match the colours of the sky.

MUD PAINTING

> Paintbrush
> Mud
> Bucket

In a bucket or other container, mix some clean dirt or earth (without stones, grass, glass, or any other particles) with water; keep the mud thin. Give your child a paintbrush and have her dip it into the mud and draw pictures or write words on the sidewalk. Be prepared: She will most likely use herself as a canvas as well! Your child will have fun hosing her creations off later, or you can leave them for the next rainfall.

WATER FIGHT

> Water balloons, water pistols, garden hose, or tub or pool of water and plastic containers

Using water balloons, water pistols, a garden hose, or a big tub or pool of water and some plastic containers, have a water fight with your child. Invite some of your child's friends over for the fun, and serve Popsicles or ice cream cones afterwards.

QUIET TIME

> Blanket
> Books
> Pillows (optional)

After lunch on a hot summer day, spread out your blanket in a shady spot under a tree. Take your child's favourite books and toys, something cool to drink, and maybe a pillow. Read, play, tell stories, or simply take a leisurely nap – both of you!

ICE BLOCKS

Water
Tempera paint
Cardboard milk cartons

Mix tempera paint with water, pour into cardboard milk cartons, and freeze to make large, colourful ice blocks. You can freeze them outside if the weather is cold enough, or use your freezer if you have the room. (If you like, make smaller blocks by freezing coloured water in clean plastic food containers or ice cube trays.) Show your child how to build a wall outside by sticking the blocks together with water. The wall will last a long time if placed out of direct sunlight and temperatures remain below freezing.

BUBBLE PIPE

Paper cup
Straw
Dish detergent
Water
Food colouring

Help your child make this simple bubble pipe. Poke a pencil hole on the side of a paper cup, one inch from the bottom, and stick a drinking straw through it, halfway into the cup. Pour dish detergent into the cup until the straw is covered. Add a little water and a few drops of food colouring. Blow gently until beautiful coloured bubbles froth over the rim of the cup and fill the air.

SLIP AND SLIDE

Garbage bags or a large sheet of plastic
Liquid dishwashing detergent
Hose or sprinkler

This is great fun for a hot day. Spread out a large sheet of plastic or a few garbage bags that have been cut open to lay flat. Pour a little bit of liquid dishwashing detergent on the plastic, then turn the hose or sprinkler on it. Your kids will have great fun getting a running start then sliding on the plastic. This works great at the foot of a slide, or on a gentle slope. Make sure to remove any rocks or other sharp objects from under the plastic.

WASH THE DISHES

> Baby bathtub or large basin
> Water
> Miscellaneous non-breakable household items
> Child's toys and play dishes
> Soap (optional)

On a warm day, set a tub of water on the deck or in the backyard and fill it with plastic cups, funnels, straws, sponges, sieves, and so on. For more fun, add a little soap. If the weather is warm enough, dress your child in her bathing suit and let her wash her toys or dishes.

MINING FOR GOLD

> Small rocks
> Gold or silver spray paint

Spray some small rocks with gold or silver spray paint to resemble gold or silver nuggets. Bury the nuggets in the dirt in your yard or sandbox, give your child a shovel, and have her dig for buried treasure. Give younger children some directions, like cold or hot, so they don't get too frustrated. Give older children a treasure map to follow.

NATURE WALK

> Notebook
> Pen or pencil
> Bird book (optional)

Take a nature walk with your child. Try to notice as many different types of trees, bugs, and birds as you can. Keep a list of what you see. If you like, bring coloured pencils and let your child draw the things she observes. If you can't identify a bug, tree, or bird, or if your child asks questions you can't answer, write down the item's description and your child's questions to look up on your next trip to the library.

MUD PIE

Sand
Dirt
Water
Bucket
Cake pan or pie plate
Grass or flower petals for decoration

Make some really good mud for your child to play with. Hand-mix sand, clean dirt, and water in a large bucket. Keep the mud really thick. Give your child a cake pan or pie plate and let her make a pie. Decorate the results of your child's efforts with grass or flower petals and bake in the sun.

BERRY PICKING

Sun screen
Sun hat
Bagged lunch
Juice
Books

Every child should pick berries at least once in her life! Kids find strawberries the easiest to pick as they are low to the ground, easy to see, and have no thorns. Find a farm that allows you to pick your own fruit. Go early in the day before it gets too hot, and don't forget the sun screen and a sun hat. Most preschoolers won't last more than half an hour at this, so take lunch, juice and some books for your child to enjoy in the shade when she tires. At home, have your child help you wash and hull the berries. Homemade jam is a marvelous project if you are feeling ambitious.

out and About

I suppose there must be in every mother's life the inevitable moment when she has to take two small children shopping in one big store.

SHIRLEY JACKSON

CHILDREN JUST NATURALLY HAVE THE DESIRE AND ENERGY TO PLAY ALL the time, but there are times when your child will just have to sit. It may be a long ride in the car, or at the doctor's, dentist's, or hairdresser's, or while you wait for your meal to arrive in a restaurant. Consider providing your child with his very own take-along Busy Bag (see Chapter 1). No matter where you are or what you are doing, being prepared with quick, easy activities that require a minimum of props will keep a cranky child calm, and a parent sane.

PORTABLE FLANNEL BOARD

> Shoe box
> Felt
> Flannel scraps
> Scissors

Cover the top of a shoe box with felt to make a small flannel board. Cut coloured felt or flannel scraps into various sizes and shapes, such as animals, cars, people, circles, squares, or triangles, or try letters and numbers if you feel ambitious. Stores the pieces in the box and take it along on your next car trip. Your child can form designs or words on the top of the shoe box using the cut-out pieces.

ADD-ON STORIES

This is a good game for the dinner table, or riding in the car. One person starts a story and each person takes a turn continuing it. You may want to have each person add a sentence, or choose a "pointer" to conduct the story. The pointer decides who goes next and can stop a person at any time, even in mid-sentence. You may want to choose a topic or theme for your story, or leave it completely open and see what kind of nonsense results.

FUN WITH WORDS

Ask your child to tell you what certain words mean to him. Pick out everyday words that he has likely heard before. Some suggestions to start you off; concrete, marriage, retire, divorce, bachelor, anniversary, occasion, special, obedient, country. You may be surprised to find that some of the words in your child's own vocabulary are something of a mystery to him. Some of the answers you get will be priceless; write them down for posterity!

WHAT AM I?

Make up riddles about animals, objects or people for your child to solve. For an elephant you could say, "I am very large; I have a long trunk; I live in Africa. What am I?" For a fire truck you may say, "I am big and red; I have a loud siren; I help put out fires. What am I?" Describe people by what they do (doctors, nurses, police officers), or friends and family by how they look (tall, wears glasses, long hair). Be specific to help your child solve the riddle without getting frustrated.

BEEP

Choose a familiar story, song, or rhyme that your child has heard often. Read or recite the story, song, or rhyme, but substitute wrong words or names in obvious places. For example: "Old MacDonald had a car," or "Mary had a little dog." Have your child listen for the incorrect words and say "Beep!" when he hears one.

MAGNET FUN

Refrigerator magnets, magnet backed letters and numbers
Cookie sheet or cake pan

This activity will help keep your little ones busy in the car when going on long trips. Bring along all the magnetic-backed toys you can find, including refrigerator magnets, magnet-backed letters, numbers, and so on. Your child can use the magnets to spell words or create pictures on the cookie sheet or cake pan.

SILLY QUESTIONS

Ask your child silly questions that will help him learn to use his imagination and make choices. For example: "Would you rather be a bird or a cow? Why?" or "Would you rather be a table or a chair? Why?" Take turns asking the questions and giving the answers.

GUESSING BAG

Pillowcase or drawstring bag
Small, unbreakable household objects

Place a variety of small, unbreakable household objects inside a bag. Close the bag so the objects are not visible. Have your child feel the objects through the bag and guess what they are.

EDIBLE NECKLACE

Shoestring licorice
Cereal or crackers with holes in the middle

Tie a knot at one end of a piece of shoestring licorice (or a plain piece of string). Show your child how to thread cereal or crackers with holes in them on the string, and then tie both ends together into a knot. The end result will amuse your child for quite some time. In the grocery store, he can eat one piece each time you put something in the cart; in the car, he can eat one piece each time he sees a dog or a red car.

FELT DOLL

    Felt
    Pen or marker
    Cardboard
    Glue
    Scissors
    Scraps of yarn and fabric
    Shoe box

Draw the shape of a person on a square of felt. The person should have clearly defined arms and legs, with the arms held away from the body. Glue the felt to a piece of cardboard and cut out the doll. Glue on yarn for hair, and draw a face with a marker. To make clothing for the doll, place the doll on scraps of fabric and use a marker to trace around the body. Cut out the clothes and dress the doll; the cloth will stick to the doll's felt body. Store the doll and clothes in a shoe box and take the box with you on long car rides.

I SEE A-B-C

While on a walk, in the car, or at the grocery store, look for objects beginning with each letter of the alphabet. If you like, make this a competition, and whoever gets to the end of the alphabet first, wins. Of course, let your child win at least some of the time!

I SPY

This word game can help develop your child's shape and colour recognition skills. As you drive or walk along, say "I spy with my little eye something that is orange," or "… something that is square." Your child will have fun guessing what it is you see. Take turns guessing what the other sees.

SOMETHING BLUE

Look around you as you wait in a doctor's office or a restaurant, or as you drive in the car. Have your child name five things that are blue, red, yellow, and so on.

CHAPTER SIX
Reading, Writing, 'rithmetic, & More

... children must be ready to learn from the first day of school. And of course, preparing children for school is a historic responsibility of parents.

GEORGE BUSH

Parents have few responsibilities more important or more rewarding than helping their child to learn. As a parent, you are your child's first and most important teacher. Children generally learn what adults around them value, and you can use your daily activities to informally teach them about reading, math, geography, and science, among other things. Children are naturally curious, and there is much you can do to advance their knowledge in these academic areas. The activities in this chapter will help you provide opportunities for your child to understand the connection between academic knowledge and the skills you use every day at home and at work.

Reading Readiness

During the preschool years, children develop at an extraordinary rate. Each day's experiences, however familiar to adults, can be fresh and exciting to curious preschoolers. Although your child's incessant curiosity may be aggravating, especially at the end of a long day, it provides an opportunity for you to help her connect daily experiences with words. Tying language to the world your child knows allows her to go beyond that world to explore new ideas. Not only do parents have abundant opportunities to help children develop language, but these opportunities often occur naturally and easily.

While connecting experience to language is an important foundation for learning to read, there is no more important activity for preparing your child to succeed as a reader than reading aloud together. When you read to your children, they almost automatically learn about written language. They learn that the words in a particular written story are always in the same order and on the same page. They may also learn that print goes from left to right, that words are made up of letters, that each letter has at least two forms (capital and small), and that there are spaces between words.

Take your child to the library on a regular basis. (The children in our family receive their very own library card when they can print their name.) Help your child find her way around the library, and show her how to look for books by her (or your) favourite authors. Appendix D provides a list of some of the best read-aloud books for young children. I also recommend *The Read-Aloud Handbook* by Jim Trelease (4th edition, Penguin Books, 1995), or *Honey for a Child's Heart* by Gladys Hunt (3rd edition, Zondervan, 1989). These books offer lots of great reading suggestions for children of all ages.

While reading with your child you will often have opportunities to answer her questions about the names, sounds, and shapes of letters. Preschoolers are very observant and often focus on company trademarks and logos that include or resemble letters of the alphabet. For example, the golden arches at McDonald's look like an M; pointing that out may be an easy way to begin. Television programs like Sesame Street also may help your child learn letters and the sounds they represent. Try to watch these shows with your child so that you can talk to her about the letters on the screen and point out all the other places those letters appear.

Research has shown that children who enter school already knowing the names and sounds of letters learn to read sooner. The following activities will help your preschooler learn to identify letters, sounds and words.

ALPHABET PLAYDOUGH

Playdough or modeling clay (see Appendix A)

Help your child form letters out of playdough or modeling clay. Then have her close her eyes, feel a letter and try to identify it by shape. As a tasty variation, make some Alphabet Cookies (see Chapter 3) and bake your alphabet!

ALPHABET MATCH-UP

Clothespins
Paper
Tape
Pen or marker
Old magazines
Scissors

Write the letters of the alphabet on small pieces of paper and tape them to clothespins, or print the letters right on the clothespins. Cut out magazine pictures, one for each letter of the alphabet, and have your child match the clothespin letters to the beginning sounds of the object in the pictures. Clip the clothespins to the corresponding pictures.

ALPHABET BOOK

Small notebook or loose sheets of paper
Crayons or markers
Old magazines
Scissors
Glue
Photos of friends and family (optional)

This is a long-term project that is great for rainy afternoons. Help your child print a letter of the alphabet on each page of a small notebook, or use loose sheets of plain or coloured paper. Your child can draw a picture of something that begins with that letter, cut pictures from old magazines and glue them onto each page, or use photographs of friends and family members.

ALPHABET PUZZLE

Index cards
Pen or markers
Scissors

Print a capital letter on the left side of an index card and the corresponding lowercase letter on the right. Cut each card into two parts with a wavy or zigzag line to make two puzzle pieces. Mix all the puzzle pieces and have your child put them together again.

DICTIONARY ZOO

There is a delightful book called *Alfred's Alphabet Walk* by Victoria Chess (Greenwillow Books, 1979) that would nicely compliment this activity.

Small notebook or loose sheets of paper
Crayons or markers
Old magazines
Scissors
Glue

This is a good rainy day project that can be completed during one or more sittings. Help your child print a letter of the alphabet on each page of a small notebook, or use loose sheets of plain or coloured paper. Have your child draw a picture of an animal that begins with that letter, or cut animal pictures from old magazines and glue them onto each page.

FIND THE LETTER

Paper
Scissors
Pen or marker
Three coffee mugs or tea cups

Cut out circles of paper small enough to hide beneath a tea or coffee cup. Write different letters on each circle. Place three tea or coffee cups on the table and hide a paper circle under only one of them. Have your child guess where the letter is and identify the letter when she finds it. Take turns hiding the circles.

GIVE ME AN "A"

Index cards or paper
Pen or marker
Tape

Print the letters of the alphabet on index cards and tape several cards onto windows, walls, furniture, and other items around the house. Tell your child what each letter is, then have her bring you the letter you ask for. Or show your child an object, such as an apple, and have her bring you the letter "A". You can also play by mixing up the cards on a table and having your child pick out the specified letters. For younger children, use fewer cards at a time.

MY NAME

Paper
Pen or marker
Clear contact paper
Crayon or marker
Damp cloth

Help your child learn to print her name. Draw two parallel solid lines with a broken line in the middle. Print your child's name (first and/or last) on the lines and cover the sheet with clear contact paper. Your child can use a crayon or marker to trace over her name and wipe it off with a damp cloth when finished.

X'S AND O'S

Paper
Pen, marker or crayons

Print one letter at the top and center of a sheet of paper. Below this, write many letters of the alphabet in no particular pattern, spreading them over the sheet of paper. Have your child circle the letters that match the one printed at the top. Have her place an "X" over the ones that do not match. For a variation, use pictures cut from old magazines and have your child identify the pictures that begin with the letter you have written.

RAISIN PLAY

Toothpicks
Raisins
Paper
Pen, crayon, or marker

Put a raisin at the tip of each toothpick; the raisins will connect the toothpicks and keep them from being easily jostled apart. On a piece of paper, draw letters and shapes that correspond in size to the toothpicks. Have your child connect the toothpicks to create each letter or shape. You may not need to draw the letters or shapes for older children. Keep in mind that your child will eat some of the raisins (which makes the activity more fun), so keep plenty on hand.

CONNECT THE DOTS

Paper
Pen or marker
Crayon

Draw a large dot-to-dot outline of your child's name on paper. Have her use a crayon to connect the dots to spell her name.

WORD RECOGNITION

Index cards
Pen or marker
Old magazines
Photographs (optional)
Scissors
Glue

Once your child can recognize the letters of the alphabet, you may want to start practicing simple word recognition. On one set of index cards, write some simple words, such as cat, dog or bird. On another set draw or cut out magazine pictures that illustrate the words you have written. Lay all the cards on the table, face up, and have your child match each word to the corresponding picture.

Try name recognition by using photographs of your child, her siblings, friends, relatives, and so on. Write the name of each person on an index card and have your child match the photo to the appropriate name.

NAME GAME

> Index cards
> Pen or marker

Print each letter in your child's name on an index card. Lay them out to spell your chid's name. Mix them up and have her try to put them back in the proper order.

CONNECT-THE-DOT ALPHABET

> Paper
> Pen, marker, or crayon

Draw a dot-to-dot outline of a simple picture. (Try tracing some pictures from your child's colouring books.) Starting with the letter A, place each letter of the alphabet at a consecutive dot. Have your child connect the dots by identifying each letter.

Mathematics

When you think about math, you probably think "arithmetic" – the adding, subtracting, multiplying and dividing you did when you first started school. The truth is that mathematics, the subject that incorporates numbers, shapes, patterns, estimation, and measurement, is much broader than that. Although we may not always realize it, math is everywhere, all around us, present in our world all the time – in the workplace, in our homes, and in life in general. Math is a very important skill, one we all need in our technological world, as well as in our everyday lives. Encourage your children to think of themselves as mathematicians who can reason and solve problems.

The good news is that most children enter school with the skills they need to succeed in math. They are curious about quantities, patterns, and shapes. In many respects, they are natural problem solvers. You can help build your child's math confidence without being an expert yourself. You can instill an interest in math in your child by doing math together — by asking questions that evoke thinking in terms of numbers and amounts and playing games that deal with such things as logic, reason, estimation, direction, classification, and time.

Teach your child that math is a part of the real world. Shopping, travelling, gardening, meal planning, cooking, eating, even laundry are all opportunities that allow you to apply math to your daily routine. Many activities throughout this book deal with cooking, sorting, patterns, and so on. Use them as well as the following activities as a fun way to help your child develop her math skills.

For additional information on children and math, I recommend *Family Math,* an excellent book packed with fun math activities for the whole family. The U.S. Department of Education also puts out a little book called *Helping Your Child Learn Math.* See Appendix E for more information on these and other helpful resources.

COUNTING

Give your child household counting assignments. Have her count all the doorknobs in the house, or all the cans in the kitchen cupboard, or all the knives, forks and spoons in the silverware drawer. You can adapt this game for outside by counting cars as you go for a walk, birds that fly by as you play on the swings, and so on.

CALENDAR MATH

Calendar
Markers or stickers (optional)

Read the calendar with your child every day. Include the weekday names, the month name, the date of the month, and the year. For example, you may say, "Today is Tuesday. That means yesterday was _____ (Monday), and tomorrow will be _____(Wednesday)", or "Today is the 10th of March. That means yesterday was the _____(9th), and tomorrow will be the _____(11th)." If possible, allow your child to place a sticker on, or mark off, each day as it is read.

NUMBER FUN

Index cards or small pieces of paper
Pen or marker
Tape

Write the numbers 1 to 10 on index cards or separate sheets of paper. Tape them on the windows around your house and ask your child to bring you a particular number. When she has mastered this, have her count objects such as the number of plates on the table, and bring you the card with the correct number.

SHAPE MATCH-UP

Coloured construction paper
White construction paper
Pen or marker
Scissors

Cut basic shapes (circle, square, rectangle, triangle, heart, and so on) out of coloured construction paper. Trace all of the shapes onto a piece of white construction paper. Have your child match the coloured shapes to those drawn on the white paper.

COUNTING PRACTICE

Ten baby food jars with lids
Hammer
Screwdriver
Marker
Dot stickers
Pennies

Hammer a wide screw driver into the baby food jar lids to make a slit big enough for a penny to fit through. Write a numeral from one to ten on the front of each jar. If your child doesn't recognize numerals, put from one to ten dot stickers on each jar. Give your child a small container of pennies and ask her to put the correct number of pennies in each jar.

WHAT'S DIFFERENT?

Various household objects

Give your child a group of objects, maybe three or four, that are related in some way: eating utensils, drawing tools, books, fruit, and so on. Add one item that doesn't fit with the rest of the objects. Have your child identify the object that doesn't belong and tell you why.

CARDS

Deck of playing cards

Pull one red card and one black card out of a deck of playing cards, and place them on the table or floor. Give your child a small stack of cards and have her practice sorting them into either the red pile or the black pile. You can also do this with each of the four suits or with the numbers on the cards.

ONE, TWO, BUCKLE MY SHOE

This familiar rhyme will help your child's counting skills. Try showing her objects in groups of one, two, three, and so on, as you recite the rhyme together.

One, two, buckle my shoe;
Three, four, close the door;
Five, six, pick up sticks;
Seven, eight, lay them straight;
Nine, ten, a big fat hen.

FOOD COUNT

Empty egg carton
Pen or marker
Small food items (raisins, cereal, chocolate chips, candies)

Write the numbers 1 to 12 on the individual sections of an egg carton. Have your child count out each number using small food items. Then have her fill the numbered section with the correct number of items. Once the sections are filled, work in reverse, having your child identify each number, count the pieces, then eat them!

NUMBER MATCH-UP

    Index cards
    Pen or marker
    Old magazines or stickers (optional)
    Scissors (optional)
    Glue (optional)

Make up two sets of index cards. On one set write numbers from one to ten, or higher. On the other set, draw (or cut out from magazines or use stickers) pictures of objects that correspond to the numbers on the first set. Lay all the cards on the table, face up, and have your child match each numbered card to the card with the corresponding number of objects.

GLITTER SHAPES

    Construction paper
    Glue
    Glitter or Colourful Creative Salt (see Appendix A)

On construction paper, use glue to draw various shapes: square, rectangle, triangle, heart, circle, oval, star. Have your child sprinkle glitter (or Colourful Creative Salt) over the shapes. Shake off the extra glitter and practice the names of each shape.

THIRTY DAYS HAS SEPTEMBER

Teach your child this rhyme about the number of days in each month:

    Thirty days has September,
    April, June and November.
    All the rest have thirty-one,
    Save February, which alone,
    Has twenty-eight and one day more,
    We add to it one year in four.

TELLING TIME

In these days of digital everything, your child may not see many conventional clocks, but telling time the "old way" is still a skill she should learn.

> Coloured construction paper
> Scissors
> Paper plate
> Paper fastener
> Crayon, pen, or marker

Make a play clock for your child to practice telling time. Cut big and little hands out of coloured construction paper and attach them to a paper plate with a paper fastener. Using a crayon, pen, or marker, number the clock appropriately. Your child can move the hands around the clock as she learns the basics of telling time. (Most young children will not learn all the details of telling time – to the quarter hour, to the minute, and so on – but, if they know their numbers up to twelve, they can certainly learn to tell time on the hour and maybe even on the half hour.)

Geography

Geography is the study of the earth, divided into five major themes: location (where it is); place (what makes a place special, both physically and culturally); interaction (between people and the environment); movement (of people, products, and information); and regions (areas defined by distinctive characteristics). Geography is a way of thinking, asking questions, observing, and appreciating the world around us.

You can help your child develop an interest in geography by providing interesting activities for her, and by prompting her to ask questions about her surroundings. To help you think geographically, and to help your child build precise mental images, try to use basic geographical terms whenever possible, i.e. west or north, climate, highway, river, and desert. Expose your child to lots of maps and let her see you using maps regularly.

The following activities are only a few examples of the many ways children learn geography. They are informal and easy to do, and are designed to help you find ways to include geographic thinking in your child's early experiences.

PLAY CITY

Markers
Large sheet of paper

Using markers on a large sheet of paper, draw an imaginary city big enough for your child's cars and trucks. Be sure to include some landmarks familiar to your child: bank, grocery store, gas station, park, hospital, school, post office, train tracks, and so on. Tape the finished city to the floor so that your child can travel around the city with her cars, trucks, and fire engines. For a more permanent city, use paints on strong cardboard or wood. Glue milk cartons or small boxes onto the map to make buildings. For a variation, make an imaginary airport or farm.

PEOPLE, PLACES, & THINGS

Maps

Go around your house and find the origins of various objects. Look at the labels of the clothes you wear and think of where your food was produced. Why do bananas come from Central America? Why does the milk come from the local dairy? Maybe your climate is too cold for bananas, and the milk is too perishable to travel far. Talk about where your ancestors came from, and use a map to find the countries. Use a map to show your child where family and friends live now.

DRAW A MAP

Paper
Pens or markers

Help your child draw a simple map of her neighbourhood. Include familiar and personal landmarks on her map: the mailbox, the store, the playground, her friend's house, the fire station. Take this map with you on your walks and point out the landmarks as you go. On your walk, collect natural materials, such as acorns and leaves, to use for an art project. At home, map the location where you found these items. You can also draw maps of your yard, your house, or your child's bedroom.

COIN & STAMP COLLECTING

> Coins and/or stamps from your own and other countries
> Small box, notebook, or coin and stamp collecting books
> Glue and tape

Start your preschooler on a coin and/or stamp collection. Ask friends and family traveling abroad to collect coins for you. Compare the coins and see what information they contain about the country. Stamps tell many different things about a country, from its political leadership to its native bird life. Show your child how to remove the stamps from your incoming mail by soaking them in a small amount of warm water. Give her special notebooks into which she can glue the stamps and tape the coins, or save them in a small box.

TREASURE HUNT

> Paper
> Pens or markers
> Small toys or other treats

Have a treasure hunt in the park, on the beach, in your backyard, or in your house. Draw a map that leads to the treasure, which can be several small toys, cars, or other items.

CLOUD WATCHING

Climate is an important part of a region's geographic character. On a warm and lazy afternoon, lay down in the grass with your child and watch the clouds drifting across the sky. Talk about how clouds are formed (water evaporates from the earth and condenses into small droplets) and what happens when clouds touch the earth (fog). Help her pick out shapes in the clouds and afterwards have her draw what she saw.

MY NEIGHBOURHOOD

Take a walk around your neighbourhood and look at what makes it unique. Point out differences from and similarities to other places. Can your child distinguish various types of homes and shops? Look at the buildings and talk about their uses. Are there features built to conform with the weather or topography? Do the shapes of some buildings indicate how they were used in the past or how they are used now? These observations help children understand the character of a place.

WHERE DO WE LIVE?

Map of your city, town or neighbourhood

Look for your city, town or neighbourhood on a map. Point out your home's location and the location of relatives' and best friends' homes. Find the school your child will attend and show your child its location in relation to your house and street. Find the nearest park, lake, mountain or other cultural or physical feature on the map and talk about how these features affect your life. Living near the ocean may make your climate moderate, prairies may provide an open path for high winds, and mountains may block some weather fronts.

LITTER PATROL

Disposing of waste is a problem with a geographic dimension.

Bag for litter
Gloves
Stick with pointed end

Go on a neighbourhood litter patrol with your child. You may want to wear gloves and use a stick with a pointed end to pick up the litter. Talk about litter, garbage and recycling and how we can help control and take care of our surroundings.

LANGUAGE PLAY

Learn simple words in different languages. Teach your child to count to 10 in other languages, and to say simple words like "hello," "goodbye," and "thank you." Have a theme day when you locate a country on the map and talk about the unique aspects of its location. Talk about the language spoken there and if possible, learn several words in that language. Serve a special lunch or snack that originated, or is popular, in that country.

NORTH, SOUTH, EAST, WEST

Small toy, book, or household object

Show your children north, south, east, and west by using your home as a reference point. If your child's bedroom faces east, point out the sun rising in the morning. Show the sunset through a window facing west. Once your child has her directional bearings, hide a small toy or household object somewhere in the house. Give directions to its location: two steps to the north, three steps west, and so on.

Basic Botany

Your child's early efforts at gardening may be clumsy, but she will be learning the basics of botany, getting dirty, and having fun all at the same time. You can teach your child how seeds develop into four basic parts – the roots, the stems, the leaves, and the flower that in turn produces new seed. She will learn that plants eat minerals through their roots, that earthworms fertilize the soil and aereate it so the roots can breathe better. Teach your child how the leaves inhale carbon dioxide and exhale oxygen, which is why nature needs a balance between animals and plants. Explain that plants are the only living things that make their own food, chlorophyll.

Use the following activities to teach your child, in an informal and fun way, the basic principles of botany.

GROWING PLANTS

Seeds
Shallow dish of water
Planters
Potting soil

Soak seeds from an orange, apple, grapefruit, lemon or lime in water for a day or two. Fill several planters with potting soil and place three or four seeds in each one about half an inch deep. Water the seeds, place the pots in a sunny spot, and watch for the green shoots to grow. You can try planting seeds in a pattern or shape: a letter, number, square, or circle.

FLOWER TINTING

This is a good activity to show your child how plants drink water through their stalks, and where the water goes.

> Clear glass or vase
> Water
> Food colouring
> White carnation or daisy

Fill a clear glass or vase halfway with water and add enough food colouring to tint the water a bright colour. Add a white carnation or daisy and watch the flower change colour over the next few hours. You can also do this experiment with celery. In fact, this may be a great way to encourage a reluctant eater. After all, purple celery is bound to taste better than the green variety!

SWEET POTATO VINE

> Sweet potato
> Toothpicks
> Glass of water
> String

Stick three toothpicks in the sides of an old sweet potato. Set it in a glass of water with the toothpicks resting on the rim of the glass. The water should just cover the tip of the sweet potato. Put the glass in a place where the vine will get filtered sunlight. Pin up some strings so the plant can climb.

CARROTS & BEETS

> Carrots or beets
> Shallow dish of water
> Small pot
> Potting soil

Cut two inches off the top of a carrot or beet. Set cut side down in a dish with half an inch of water. Change the water every day or two. When roots appear plant your carrot or beet, cut side down, in a pot of moist soil. Set it in a sunny window and keep it wet.

AvocADo TREE

Avocado seed
5" pot
Potting soil

Dry the avocado seed for a couple of days, then peel the papery brown skin off. Plant, base down, about two-thirds down in a pot of soil, leaving the pointed tip exposed until the seed germinates (30 to 90 days). You can keep this in the sun, or well-watered in a dark cupboard for a stronger root system. When the seed sprouts, leave one new shoot at the top and pinch off the rest of the new growth. This will allow all the plant's energy to go into the one remaining shoot, which should then grow into a lush, bushy tree.

GARLic CLoVE

Garlic clove
Potting soil
Small pot

Plant an unpeeled garlic clove in potting soil, pointed end up. Cover completely, water every few days, and keep in the sun.

LIMA BEAN SPROUTS

Lima beans
Shallow dish
Water

Put lima beans in a dish and fill with water. Place the dish in a sunny window and watch how the beans change daily.

CHAPTER SEVEN

Music, Dance, & Drama

The events of childhood do not pass, but repeat themselves like seasons of the year.

ELEANOR FARJEON

MUSIC, DANCE, AND DRAMA ARE AN ESSENTIAL PART OF OUR children's general education. Through the study of music, dance and drama, children acquire knowledge, skills, and attitudes that influence them throughout their lives. In addition to learning music for its own sake, children who participate in music learn coordination, goal-setting, concentration, and cooperation. Dance activities also offer many benefits for children, encouraging mental and emotional development while enhancing motor skills. Drama involves mind, body, and imagination, and is essential to a child's full development.

This chapter provides simple ideas that will help you stimulate your child's development in these three areas. The following activities will cultivate your child's sense of rhythm, allow your child to experience movement as it relates to music and rhythm, and encourage your child in creative play.

Music & Rythm

As a parent, you can encourage your child's love of music and nurture his musical talents in a number of ways: listen to good music programs and recordings together, attend musical events, make music as a family, and praise children for their musical activities and accomplishments. As a result of music-listening and music-making experiences, children can become better listeners and develop musical intelligence.

Listening to music, moving to music, and playing musical games are the best musical activities for young children. The following ideas will help you begin to develop your child's sense of music and rhythm.

SHAKERS

> Plastic medicine bottles in various sizes, soap bottles, small pop-top juice cans, or small aluminum pie or tart pans
> Popcorn, rice, dried beans, pennies, and other noise-making items
> Glue gun or tape

Collect an assortment of variously sized plastic medicine bottles, soap bottles, small juice cans, or small aluminum pie or tart pans. Partially fill each with anything that creates noise: popcorn, rice, dried beans, pennies, and so on. Use a variety of items, as each makes a different sound. If the container has a lid, or if using aluminum pie pans, secure them with glue from a hot glue gun. If the container doesn't have a lid, tape it shut.

TAMBOURINE

> Corn kernels, dried beans, small pasta, cereal, and so on
> Two paper plates
> Glue or staples
> Hole punch
> Ribbon
> Crayons, markers, stickers for decoration

Place corns, beans, pasta, or cereal onto a paper plate, cover with the second plate, and glue or staple the rims of the plates together. When the glue is dry, punch holes around the rims and lace ribbon through the holes. Let your child decorate with crayons, markers, stickers, and so on.

COFFEE CAN DRUM

> Empty coffee can with two plastic lids
> Contact paper or your child's artwork

Glue
Pencil
Empty thread spool

Create a drum for your child by cutting the bottom out of an empty coffee can. Cover the can with contact paper (or let your child draw a picture on some paper and glue the paper around the can). Glue plastic lids on each end of the can. Create a drumstick by gluing the lead end of a pencil into the hole of an empty thread spool.

For a variation, an empty paper towel roll and an empty oatmeal box will make a soft but authentic drum for your preschooler.

MILK CARTON GUITAR

Cardboard milk carton (two litre size)
Tape
Sharp knife
Yardstick
Saw
45" length of nylon fishing line

Make a guitar that your child can really play! Tape shut the top of a clean, empty milk carton. With a sharp knife, cut vertical slits, big enough to slip a yardstick through, in two sides of the carton, two-thirds up from the bottom. Cut a notch about a half inch deep near each end of the yardstick and insert through the carton. Position the carton near the centre of the yardstick. Make a loop in one end of the length of fishing line and slip it over the notch on the top of the yardstick. Pull the line over the top of the carton and loop it around the notch at the other end of the yardstick. Tie securely and pull the carton to one end of the yardstick. To play the guitar, strum the string near the top edge of the milk carton with one hand. Pinch the string to the yardstick with the other hand to change pitches.

SANDPAPER BLOCKS

Two 4" pieces of a two-by-four piece of wood
Sandpaper
Glue

Glue sandpaper onto the wood, and rub together for an interesting sound.

RHYTHM BLOCKS

Two 4" pieces of a two-by-four piece of wood

Give your child two pieces of wood to use as rhythm blocks; make sure that the blocks are smooth and the edges are not too sharp. Your child can bang them together in time to a rhythmic beat.

NOISE BLOWER

Empty cardboard toilet paper tube
Wax paper
Elastic band
Crayons, markers, stickers, fabric, construction paper, and other
    items for decoration

Cover one end of a cardboard toilet paper tube with a piece of wax paper, using an elastic band to hold the wax paper in place. Blow and hum into the uncovered end to make a vibrating sound. Older children can make this for themselves, decorating the tube with crayons, markers, stickers, or scraps of ribbon, fabric, or construction paper.

PIE PLATE TAMBOURINE

Aluminum pie plate
Hammer and nail
6 to 8 flattened bottle caps
String

Using a hammer and nail, an adult should make six to eight holes around the edge of an aluminum pie plate, and one hole in the centre of the same number of flattened bottle caps. Let your child pull a piece of string through each bottle cap and thread it through a hole in the pie plate. Tie a knot tight enough to hold the bottle cap in place, but allow enough slack so that the cap can move freely and hit the pie plate when shaken. Attach each cap in this way; shake to play.

Movement & Dance

For young children, dance offers an avenue for exploration, discovery, and the development of natural instincts for movement. Dance has many physical benefits — among them increased flexibility, improved circulation, development of muscle tone and strength, and improved posture, balance, and coordination. But although dance can be great exercise and an artistic expression of mind and body, for young children dance is usually just plain fun. It's also a great way to help children "shake their sillies out"!

LET'S PRETEND

Have your child tell a story by acting it out with body movements, or ask him to move with different types of walks (downhill, on parade, stiff, up stairs) or pretend to use different kinds of vehicles (bicycle, skateboard, car, horse, and so on). This will provide your child with the opportunity to explore and invent movement.

MOVING QUESTIONS

Ask your child questions like, "How many ways can you balance yourself besides standing?" and "How many different ways can you move your head (arms, leg, upper body)?" Questions like these will help your child become aware of his body and its relationship to other people and the environment.

MUSIC & MOVEMENT

Homemade rhythm instruments, real musical instruments such as a piano or guitar, or recorded music

The goal of this activity is to have your child experience movement as it relates to music or rhythm. Play different types of music and have your child physically express how the music makes him feel: run for fast music, tiptoe for soft music, hop and bounce for happy music, march for a parade tune, and so on. You can also tap out a rhythmic beat and encourage your child to clap or hop in time to the beat.

EXERCISE CLASS

Pretend to have an exercise class in your living room. You can dress in exercise wear if you like, and take turns being the "instructor". Include both locomotor movements (walking, running, jumping, skipping, and so on) and non-locomotor movements (bending, stretching, twisting, swinging, and so on). Vary the size, level, and direction of these basics to allow your child to discover a large number of movements that can be combined to form basic dance steps. You can also make a point of including these movements in other games you play, such as Simon Says or Follow the Leader (Chapter 2).

CIRCLE DANCES

Circle dances are a great way to stress body movement. Whether you dance with several children or just one, circle dances can be a lot of fun. Try old favourites like Hokey Pokey, Looby Loo, Ring Around the Rosie, Mulberry Bush, Skip to My Lou, or London Bridge. For more ideas, your local library will likely have song books, cassettes or videos by many popular children's performers.

Dramatic Play

Children of all ages love to pretend. As toddlers, they first enter the world of make-believe by engaging in activities they see around them and by putting themselves in the place of others. This activity involves mind, body, and imagination. It is a child's rehearsal for life and is essential to a child's full development.

As children grow older, their play develops more structure. They act out favourite stories, create original situations from life experiences, and imagine themselves in fantasy worlds where anything is possible. If they are encouraged in this kind of play at home, they become ready for creative drama by the time they enter school.

The following activities will encourage your child's dramatic play.

TICKLE TRUNK

>   Empty trunk or large box
>   Dress-up clothes and props

You can encourage your child's dramatic play by setting up a Tickle Trunk full of props for him. Fill a trunk or box with adult clothes, shoes, hats, scarves, gloves, and costume jewelry to use for dress-up. Old suits are great, as are Hawaiian shirts, vests, baseball hats, bridesmaid dresses, nightgowns, wigs, boots, slippers, and purses. Great items can be found at garage sales or local thrift shops. A Tickle Trunk will be an invaluable part of your child's dramatic play and items can be added for years.

POST OFFICE

>   Unopened "junk mail"
>   Unused return envelopes from your mail
>   Stickers from magazine and record clubs
>   Inexpensive stationery
>   One-cent stamps
>   Bank slips
>   Date stamp or other rubber stamp and ink pad

Help your child open up a post office of his own. Save unopened junk mail, unused return envelopes from mail you receive, and stickers from magazine and record clubs. You may want to provide him with inexpensive stationery and authentic one-cent stamps. Give him a date stamp or other rubber stamp and inkpad, and bank slips for official looking forms.

RESTAURANT

>   Tablecloth or other linens
>   Vase with flowers or other centrepiece
>   Candle (optional)
>   Menu

Use table linens, flowers (real or other) in a vase, and a candle. Take the customer's coat, show him to his seat, give him a menu, and let him order lunch or dinner. Take turns being the waiter and the customer.

HoSPITAL

    Stuffed animals
    Pillows
    Blankets
    White clothes for uniforms
    Thermometer
    Bandages
    Medicine measuring spoon
    Sling (flat cloth diaper or other material folded into a triangle)

Using friends, stuffed animals, or cooperative parents for patients, help your child set up a hospital or doctor's office. Lay pillows and blankets in a corner of the room. Give the "nurse" or "doctor" white clothing for his uniform. Show him how to take temperatures with a thermometer, bandage arms and legs, and give medicine. Make a sling from a flat cloth diaper or other piece of material folded into a triangle. Take turns playing the part of doctor, nurse, patient, and visitor.

BEAUTY SALoN

    Brushes
    Curlers
    Hair bows
    Empty hair spray bottle filled with water
    Towel
    Nail polish (optional)

Give your child brushes, curlers, hair bows, and an empty hair spray bottle filled with water to use in his beauty salon. Use friends, siblings, or parents for clients, and take turns being the hairdresser. Use a towel to absorb water used during play. For girls, apply nail polish on fingers and toes as a special treat.

GRoCERY SToRE

    Empty food boxes, plastic containers, unbreakable jars
    Old purse or wallet
    Play money

Scissors
Store coupons
Grocery list
Paper grocery bag

Help your child set up a grocery store by saving empty boxes, plastic containers, unbreakable jars, and so on. Give him an old purse or wallet containing play money and coins. He can practice his cutting skills by cutting out your unwanted coupons to use in his store. Help him make up a shopping list and give him a bag for his groceries.

BARBER SHOP

Brushes and combs
Empty hair spray bottle filled with water
Shaving cream
Popsicle stick or old credit card
Towel

Help your child set up a barber shop. Give him brushes, combs, an empty hair spray bottle filled with water, and shaving cream. A wooden Popsicle stick or old credit card can be used as a razor. Use a towel to wipe off shaving cream and water. Take turns being the barber.

DENTIST

Cup with water
Bowl for spitting
Paper napkin
Flashlight
Toothbrush
Small toys for "prizes"

Because water is involved, this game is best played in the kitchen or bathroom. Take turns being the dentist and patient. The dentist tucks a paper napkin into the patient's collar to protect his shirt, then uses the flashlight to look into his mouth. The dentist may want to brush the patient's teeth, then advise him to rinse his mouth and spit into the bowl. As the patient leaves, be sure the dentist can offer him a "prize".

BAKERY

Apron
White paper lunch bag
Rolling pin
Cookie cutters
Playdough
Prepared cookie dough (optional)
Plastic knife or Popsicle stick (optional)
Cookie sheet (optional)

Put on an apron and wear a white paper lunch bag on your head for a baker's hat. With a rolling pin and cookie cutters, "bake" cookies, pies, and cakes out of playdough. Or use a roll of prepared cookie dough: give your child a plastic knife or Popsicle stick, have him slice off cookies, and place them on a cookie sheet for real baking.

CHAPTER EIGHT

Arts & Crafts

The parents exist to teach the child, but also they must learn what the child has to teach them; and the child has a very great deal to teach them.

ARNOLD BENNETT

ART AND CRAFT PROJECTS PROVIDE GREAT OPPORTUNITY FOR CREATIVE play for your child. Through her work with arts and crafts, your child will learn to think creatively and develop skills in drawing, painting, sculpting, designing, and crafting. Well-chosen art and craft projects will help your child develop concentration and coordination, as well as organizational and manipulative skills. They will promote a sense of great achievement, and are fun and exciting for children of all ages.

That said, one of the main problems I've always had with art and craft projects is, what do you do with all the wonderful things your child so busily and happily creates? Children can produce an enormous volume of work in a short amount of time. Multiply that by two or three children and you can have a major problem on your hands! Here are some ideas that might help:

Always be on the alert for creative ways to use your child's art, i.e. as gifts or giftwrap (see Appendix C).

Display your child's art around the house, not just on the refrigerator. Visit an art framing shop and ask them to save their mat scraps for you. You may get some pieces that are great for either mounting or framing your child's work.

Make Grandma or other relatives a calendar of your child's art. Save your little artist's work throughout the year. As the new year approaches, visit local businesses and collect free calendars. Glue your child's art onto the picture part of each month, so a new masterpiece will be displayed each time the calendar changes.

Create a "portfolio" for your child. Using a 3-ring binder and plastic page protectors, save some of your child's outstanding creations. Be sure to date or write your child's age on each work of art. For extra large or 3-D projects, take a photo or two and put those in the binder. (The project itself will have to go eventually!).

When the day comes (and it will) to get rid of some of the pictures and projects your child has created, be sure to do it in a sensitive way. Chances are she will not miss that picture that was hanging on the refrigerator for a month, but finding it crumpled up in the kitchen waste basket is sure to make her feel that you don't really value her work. Take items directly to the outdoor trash containers just before the garbage is picked up to save you and your child some heartache.

Old phone books come in very handy for children's little projects. When your child is colouring, painting, or gluing, open the phone book and place your child's paper on a clean page. Then simply turn the page for a clean working surface for the next project. This way, you won't have to worry about finding scrap paper to line your child's work space, and you won't have to clean paint and glue off your kitchen table nearly as often.

Here are some activities you can use to introduce your child to the world of art. Remember that your own attitudes make strong impressions on your child; encourage her to experiment. Art and craft projects are a form of self-expression and your child should know that there is no right or wrong way to create art.

Drawing

Drawing is probably the first art form your child will experience. It allows your child to express herself creatively and helps the development of small muscles and hand/eye coordination. Drawing is simple and it can be done anywhere and at anytime. It is something that most of us do, in some form or another, all our lives.

Give your child a little variety in her drawing tools and materials. Try using pens, pencil crayons, chalk, and markers. For drawing paper, use construction paper, newspaper, fine sandpaper, or cut-open grocery bags in varying sizes. Your child will also enjoy drawing on shapes such as circles, triangles, and stars cut from different types of paper.

STAINED GLASS CRAYONS

Warning: These do come out looking a little like peanut butter cups. Your child just may decide to take a bite!

> Broken crayon pieces
> Muffin tin, greased
> Aluminum foil (optional)

This is a good project to use up all those broken crayon pieces. Remove any paper from the crayons and place the pieces in a well-greased muffin tin (or line the tin with aluminum foil). Place the tin in a 400-degree oven for a few minutes, until the crayons have melted. Remove from the oven and cool completely before removing from the tin. If you have mixed crayon colours in the tin, the circles will have a stained glass effect and are great for colouring.

RAINBOW CRAYONS

Beautiful, and easy for little hands to hold!

> Broken crayon pieces
> Clean, empty tin cans
> Pot of hot water
> Empty, plastic 35-mm film canister

This is another good way to use broken crayons. Remove any paper from the crayons and sort them by colour. Place the pieces, one colour at a time, in the empty tin cans. Set the tin cans in a pot of very hot or boiling water until the crayons have melted. Pour a small amount (approximately a quarter inch) into each film canister. When the wax hardens, add a second colour in the same way. When you are done, you will have a crayon rainbow of layered colours.

CLOTHESPIN CRAYONS

Clothespins
Crayons
Paper

Clip a clothespin around a crayon and encourage your child to draw while holding onto the clothespin instead of the crayon. The idea is to try to do the same old things in new and different ways. Clipping a clothespin onto a crayon will make colouring seem different and interesting, if only for a few minutes.

THUMBPRINT MICE

Stamp pad
Paper
Crayons or markers

Have your child press her thumb on a stamp pad and then press it onto paper. Show your child how to draw a mouse tail and ears on the thumbprint to complete each mouse. Do this several times to make a mouse family. Use your own thumb and perhaps one of an older or younger sibling, then compare the different sizes each makes.

RAINBOW DRAWING

Crayons
Tape
Paper

Tape two or more crayons together and have your child draw a picture. You will get some interesting effects with this double and triple layering of colour. If you want to use true rainbow colours you will need violet, indigo, blue, green, yellow, orange, and red.

SELF-PORTRAITS

Very large sheet of newsprint or other paper
Markers, crayons, or paint

Have your child lie down on the floor on the paper. Trace around her, then let her fill in the details with markers, paint, or crayons. Tell her to be as detailed as possible: What is her hair like? What colour are her eyes? What clothes is she wearing? When finished, hang her portrait in her room or on her door where she can admire it.

FRUIT RUB

Cardboard
Scissors
Paper
Paper clips
Crayons

Cut a fruit shape, such as an apple, orange, or banana out of cardboard. Place the cardboard shape between two sheets of paper and clip them together with a paper clip. Give your child an appropriately coloured crayon, and have her rub over the paper lightly to make a red apple or yellow banana appear.

NATURE COLOURS

Plants and flowers collected on a walk
Crayons
Paper

Go on a walk with your child and bring home a variety of plants and flowers, such as grass, leaves, dandelions, and so on. Spread them out on a table in your backyard and encourage your child to draw a picture using only crayons in colours that match the items you have collected.

BARK DRAWING

Tree bark
Crayons, pens, or paint

Go for a walk and collect tree bark. At home, use crayons, pens, or paint to draw pictures on the bark. Talk about how people used tree bark before paper was invented, and how paper comes from trees.

PICTURE A STORY

Paper
Crayons or markers

Have your child draw a series of four or five pictures. Have her then dictate a story to go with each picture. You can write it on the bottom of the picture as it is told.

CRAYON RUBBINGS

Paper or cut-open grocery bags
Small textured objects
Crayons

Place paper or cut-open grocery bags over textured objects such as leaves, string, doilies, paper clips, fabric, tiles, coins, cardboard shapes, or bricks. Rather than use the end of a crayon, have your child rub the flat side of a crayon on the paper. Shift the paper and use different colours for interesting patterns.

WET CHALK DRAWINGS

6 Tbsp. sugar
¼ cup water
Coloured chalk
Paper

Mix together sugar and water and pour over chalk; let soak for ten minutes. Have your child use the wet chalk to draw on white paper. If you use white chalk, draw on coloured paper.

SECRET MESSAGES

White crayon or wax candle
Paper
Tempera paints
Paintbrush

Use a white crayon or wax candle to write a message or draw a picture on a piece of white paper. Your child can then paint over the paper with tempera paint to see the picture or message.

HAND DRAWINGS

Paper
Crayons or markers
Nail polish (optional)
Sparkles or small beads
Glue

Place your child's hands on a piece of paper and trace around them. Give your child crayons, markers or nail polish and have her paint the nails of her drawing. Use glue and sparkles or small beads to add rings, watches, and other details. For variety, try tracing your child's feet, then have her trace your feet and compare sizes. Colour the feet and add nail polish and funny rings with crayons or markers.

BLINDFOLD DRAWING

Blindfold
Crayons or markers
Paper

Place a blindfold on your child, then have her draw on paper with crayons or markers. When her drawing is complete, remove the blindfold and take turns looking for hidden shapes or objects in the picture.

SCRIBBLE DRAWING

Paper
Crayons

Show your child how to scribble on a piece of white paper with a crayon, using big circular motions to form loops. Then have your child colour in each loop with a different colour, creating a very pretty and unique design every time.

Painting

Painting is a wonderful outlet for a child's creativity. Large pieces of art paper, pots of paint in vivid colours, big paintbrushes, and a painter's smock will keep your little artist happy on many a rainy afternoon. Provide a good work space, keep supplies handy, and make clean-up part of the project. Work outdoors when you can and let nature provide further inspiration.

The best kind of paint for young children is poster paint, also known as tempera paint, which you can buy at any art store in pre-mixed liquid form, or as a powder that must be mixed with water. You can also make your own poster paint using the recipes in Appendix A. Children rarely need more than three colours: red, blue, and yellow. Teach your child how to mix these colours to create others. Tempera blocks are also available; they are practical because they don't have to be diluted and can't be spilled, making cleanup easier. In addition, tempera blocks are economical, since they are less expensive and last a very long time; however, your child will probably not find them as fun as the slick liquid paints.

Paper can be purchased from an art supply store, but consider some of the following alternatives. Newsprint is a wonderful paper for painting; roll-ends can be purchased cheaply from a newspaper publisher. Visit your local printer and ask if you can leave an empty box for a week or two; she may agree to fill it with all kinds of wonderful paper that would otherwise be discarded. Try fine sandpaper as an alternative art paper for a wonderful effect. For fingerpainting, use the shiny side of freezer paper that can be purchased at the grocery store. It is much cheaper than special fingerpaint paper and works just as well.

String up a line in the laundry room or kitchen that can be used to hang paintings to dry. Wet artwork can be attached to the line with clothespins. When dry, be sure to display your child's paintings prominently. And think of creative uses for some of her work; many painting projects make wonderful gift-wrap or greeting cards.

STARCH PAINTING

> Bowl
> Liquid starch
> Liquid detergent
> Powdered tempera paint

Mix a small amount of detergent with liquid starch and put on a painting surface such as a table top, paper, or plastic cloth. Sprinkle powdered tempera paint over the starch, and allow your child to experiment with mixing colours.

DIPPING

> Paper towel
> Bowls of diluted food colouring or strong watercolours

Have your child fold a piece of paper towel into a fairly small packet. Have her dip each corner of the packet into a bowl of coloured dye, which can be either diluted food colouring or strong watercolours. Use a different colour for each corner. Unfold the paper towel and hang to dry. You can use various types of paper; the more absorbent the paper, the faster the dye will spread. Dipped rice paper makes a nice gift wrap, but it is fairly expensive.

FINGERPAINTING

> Fingerpaints
> Paper

Fingerpainting is a wonderfully messy adventure that every child should experience after about the age of two (younger, if you can stand it!). Unfortunately, it can be a frustrating experience for parents, as the amount of work required to set up and clean up never seems to merit the five minutes (or less) most children will spend at this activity! That said, be prepared for a great big mess, and make sure your child wears an art smock. Wet the paper first to allow the paint to slide better, drop a blob of paint on the paper and let your child go to it. Commercial fingerpaint can be bought, or make your own using the recipes in Appendix A.

STRING PAINTING

Paper
Liquid tempera paint
String or yarn

Drop some paint onto a piece of paper and let your child make a design by dragging string through the paint and around the paper. Try it again by dipping the string in the paint and dragging it across the paper. Use different types and lengths of string and yarn for varying effects.

AIR PAINTING

Paper
Liquid tempera paint
Empty squeeze bottle

Have your child drop some paint onto a piece of paper and disperse it by squeezing air onto it with an empty squeeze bottle. She can also do this by blowing on the paint through a wide plastic tube or straw. If you like, add a second and third colour. You can also try different types of paper for different effects.

BALLOON PAINTING

Balloons in various sizes
Liquid tempera paint
Paper

Blow up balloons of various sizes and tie the ends. Hold onto the tied end, dip the balloon into liquid tempera paint, and blot it onto a sheet of paper. The resulting artwork can be displayed on the wall or used as unique gift-wrap.

DRIPPY PAINTING

Paper or a cut-open brown paper bag
Liquid tempera paint
Eyedropper, spoon or straw

On a big sheet of art paper or a cut-open brown paper bag, have your child drip liquid tempera paints using an eyedropper, spoon, or straw. Tip the paper in different directions to make a design. Drip another colour and tip the paper again for an interesting result.

BUBBLE PAINTING

> Newspaper
> Liquid dishwashing detergent
> Shallow dish
> Tempera paint
> Straw
> Construction paper or other paper

Cover your child's work surface with newspaper. Pour a quarter cup liquid dishwashing detergent into a shallow dish. If you use powdered tempera, mix a small amount of water with the paint. Add paint mixture or liquid tempera to the dishwashing liquid until the colour is intense. Place one end of a straw into the mixture, and blow until the bubbles are almost billowing over the edge of the dish. Gently place a piece of construction paper or other paper on top of the bubbles and hold it in place until several bubbles have popped. Continue this process with different colors, blowing more bubbles as needed. To make a unique greeting card, use a piece of construction paper folded in half. When dry, your child can add drawings to the picture and sign her name.

3-D STRING PAINTING

> Bowl
> Liquid tempera paint
> Liquid starch
> String
> Paper

For this activity, mix liquid tempera paint and liquid starch in equal parts in a bowl. Dip some string into the paint/starch solution and drop it onto a sheet of paper. When the paint dries, the starch will make the string stick to the paper.

EYEDROPPER PAINTING

Eyedropper
Liquid tempera paint
Paper

Show your child how to use an eyedropper and some liquid tempera paint to drop paint onto paper to make a picture. Use different colours, if you like, and be sure to put the painting on display when dry.

SPRAY PAINTING

Newspaper
Paper or a cut-open brown paper bag
Tempera paint
Plant sprayer

For this activity you will want to prepare your work area well. Lay down lots of newspaper, and be prepared to offer close supervision. Place some art paper or cut-open brown paper bags on the newspaper. Pour some thin paint into a plant sprayer and let your child spray it onto the paper. Use several different colours, and when the paper is dry you will have some great gift-wrap.

STENCIL PAINTING

Thin cardboard
Scissors
Paper
Tape
Sponge or brush
Liquid tempera paint

Draw a design, letter, or animal shape on thin cardboard. Cut out the inside of the shape to make the stencil, and tape the stencil onto a sheet of paper. Show your child how to dip a sponge or brush into liquid tempera paint, then fill in the inside of the stencil with colour. When finished, remove the tape and lift off the stencil to see the design.

PAINT BLOT ART

Construction paper
Liquid tempera paint
Spoon
Rolling pin

Fold a piece of construction paper in half like a greeting card, then open it up. Using liquid tempera paints and a spoon, have your child drop different colours onto one of the inside halves of the paper. Fold the paper again with the paint on the inside, and have your child roll a rolling pin over the paper to spread the paint. Open up the paper and have your child use her imagination to decide what the blot looks like. When the paint is dry, fold the paper so that the paint is on the outside. Use as a unique greeting card.

MARBLE PAINTING

Marbles
Liquid tempera paint
Paper

Have your child drop marbles into various colours of paint and roll them across a piece of paper. You may want to set up some barriers around the paper, or place the paper and marbles inside a flat box (the kind a 24-pack of pop comes in), to prevent the marbles from rolling off and creating a mess.

TOOTHPICK PAINTING

Toothpicks
Liquid tempera paint
Paper
Glue

Give your child toothpicks to dip into tempera paint and use as a paintbrush. When the paint dries, she can glue the toothpicks onto her painting for a three-dimensional effect.

PAINT PEN

Empty roll-on deodorant bottle
Liquid tempera paint

To make a giant paint pen for your child, pry off the top of a roll-on deodorant bottle. Fill the bottle with tempera paint, and snap on the top. Your child can use this tool to draw pictures, practice her letters and numbers, or create abstract designs.

TENNIS BALL PAINTING

Okay, this one takes courage, but it's a lot of fun (and best done outdoors)!

Newspaper
Paper
Tennis balls
Liquid tempera paint

Spread newspapers on the sidewalk or another firm surface, and place a large sheet of paper on top of the newspapers. Dip tennis balls, a different one for each colour, into liquid tempera paint and bounce them onto the paper for a great painting effect.

FOOT PAINTING

Newspaper
Fingerpaint paper or other paper
Liquid tempera paint or fingerpaint
Warm, soapy water in a bucket
Towel
Rubber boots or tennis shoes (optional)

Cover your floor with newspaper, then spread large sheets of fingerpaint paper or other paper on the newspapers. Pour about a quarter cup liquid tempera paint or fingerpaint onto the glossy side of the paper, if using fingerpaint paper. Encourage your bare-footed child to walk, stamp, and slide her feet through the paint to make different effects. Have a bucket of warm, soapy water and a towel ready for clean up. For a variation, have your child wear rubber boots or tennis shoes.

NEGATIVE PAINTING

Textured objects
Glue
Paper
Tempera paint
Paintbrush or toothbrush (optional)

Gather together a collection of interesting objects, such as lace doilies, paper dolls, leaves, or letters, numbers or shapes, cut out of cardboard. Have your child place a dab of glue on one or more objects and stick it to a white piece of paper. Then tell her to paint over the paper and the shape. When the paint is dry, remove the shape to see the negative image. You can make a unique greeting card by folding the paper in half and painting on one side.

For a different effect, place the objects on a piece of paper and have your child spatter paint over them using a paintbrush or toothbrush. Remove the objects from the paper and show your child the negative images that appear.

WINDOW STENCILING

Leaves in different shapes and sizes
Masking tape
Sponge
Clothespins
Liquid tempera paint (orange, yellow, red and brown)
Newspaper

On a fall walk with your child, collect several different types and colours of leaves. At home, attach rolled pieces of masking tape to the backsides of the leaves and arrange them on the window in the way you want them to appear in stenciled form. Make sure the leaves lay flat against the glass. Dip small pieces of sponge clipped onto clothespins into liquid tempera paints in fall colours. Blot on newspaper to absorb excess paint, then lightly dab the sponge around the edge of each leaf. Use a new piece of sponge for each colour. When the paint is dry, carefully remove the leaves, leaving the outlines on the window. The leaf patterns can be easily removed with window cleaner or soap and water.

Printmaking

Young children can experience a sense of great accomplishment with printmaking. Not only is printmaking fun, but it allows a young child to achieve an attractive reproduction of an object without a great amount of artistic skill or coordination. Through the repetition of an impression, children can develop an appreciation of texture and design.

Printmaking involves making an impression of an object onto paper or another surface. The object to be printed can be covered in paint using a brush or a paint roller, be dipped into paint, or pressed on a print pad.

A print pad can be made by padding up newspaper and soaking it in liquid tempera paint. Or place a thin sponge in a shallow tray or small bowl and cover with several tablespoons of paint. For some printmaking, a rubber stamp pad can also be used. To cushion the print, place a newspaper under the paper on which the impression is to be made.

Many different types of paper can be used for printing; newsprint, construction paper, and cut-open brown paper bags are some of the cheaper options. As with many of the painting projects in this chapter, you can use these printing activities to create some great, environmentally friendly gift-wrap.

FRUIT AND VEGETABLE PRINTING

> Various fruit and vegetables
> Paring knife
> Print pad or stamp pad
> Paper

Cut fruits and vegetables into halves, quarters, circles, or any other shapes, and dip into tempera paints or on a print or stamp pad, and then press onto plain or coloured paper. Apples cut in half will have a star design in the middle (where the seeds are), while green peppers make a great shamrock design. Cut a potato in half and use a small paring knife to create a relief design: circles, square, hearts, and so on. If you make letters, don't forget to carve them backwards so they will print correctly.

PLAYDOUGH PRINTING

Playdough
Tools for making a design (pencil, bottle camp, cookie cutter, cooking utensils)
Print pad
Paper

Roll playdough into a ball and flatten it until it is about two inches thick. On one side of the dough, press in a design using a pencil, bottle cap, cookie cutter, or other cooking utensil. Gently press the playdough onto the print pad then onto paper. Repeat using various colours and designs.

STRING BLOCK PRINTING

String or rope
Small blocks of wood
Liquid tempera paint
Shallow pan
Paper

Wrap string or rope several times around a small block of wood. Tie it in place (make sure the rope is distributed evenly over the block, not gathered in one spot). Have your child press the string block into liquid tempera paint then press onto paper. She should move the block around in different directions and add different colours to vary the design.

FINGERPAINT PRINTS

Fingerpaint
Plastic tabletop
Large sheets of paper

Commercial fingerpaint can be purchased, or you can make your own using the fingerpaint recipes in Appendix A. Place a small amount of fingerpaint onto a plastic tabletop and have your child mess around until her design is complete. Have her wash and dry her hands thoroughly, then place a large sheet of paper on top of the fingerpainting. Rub all over the back of the paper with clean, dry hands. Slowly lift the paper off the table and hang to dry.

GADGET PRINTING

½ inch softwood cubes or matchboxes
Small objects in interesting shapes (matchsticks, string, wood chips,
    curtain rings, bottle caps, or cardboard shapes)
Glue
Print pad or stamp pad
Paper

Glue interesting shapes onto half-inch softwood cubes or matchboxes; matchsticks, string, wood chips, curtain rings, keys, bottle caps, or shapes cut from cardboard are just a few examples. You can make letter or number stamps on wood cubes by drawing the image in reverse, then chipping away the surface except for the shape to be printed. Or use larger objects, such as a potato masher, fly swatter, or salt shaker. Press the object onto the print pad or rubber stamp pad and stamp it on the paper, varying colours and objects to create unique designs.

RoLLER PRINTING

Thin foam
Scissors
Glue
Empty toilet paper or paper towel roll
Liquid tempera paint
Shallow pan
Paper or cut-open brown paper bags

Cut out some interesting shapes from thin pieces of foam. Stars are nice, or make hearts, Christmas trees, or other season-appropriate shapes. Glue the shapes onto empty paper towel or toilet paper rolls. Pour some liquid tempera paint into a shallow pan big enough to fit the paper roll. Dip the "roller" into the paint, then roll onto a sheet of paper or cut-open brown paper bag.

For a variation on this, use a real foam paint roller. At even intervals, tie the roller with string. This will make stripes when dipped in paint and pressed on paper. Or cut chunks out of the roller to make a thick solid pattern with holes in it.

PAPER BATIK

    Construction paper
    Crayons
    Liquid tempera paint
    Paintbrush
    Newspaper
    Paper
    Hot iron

Have your child completely colour a piece of construction paper with crayons. Show her how to crumple the paper carefully into a tight ball, then gently unfold the picture and notice how the surface has cracked. Brush contrasting liquid tempera paint over the paper to create a mosaic effect. When the picture dries, place it on a sheet of newspaper and cover it with a piece of thin paper. Using a patting motion, iron over the paper with a hot iron to smooth the wrinkles and to transfer the original image to the blank paper.

CRAYON MELT PRINTS

This activity requires the use of a food warming tray or electric griddle. Close supervision by an adult is recommended.

    Food warming tray or electric griddle
    Aluminum foil
    Crayons
    Oven mitts
    Damp cloth

Cover the food warming tray or electric griddle with aluminum foil. Set on low setting and when the tray is warm, have your child make a drawing on the foil with crayon. The crayon will melt as she draws and produce beautiful, colourful designs. To make a print, lay a sheet of paper over the crayon design and carefully smooth the paper down with oven mitts. Lift it off and see the design transferred onto the paper. Wipe the foil clean with a damp cloth and start again for a new print.

MESH PRINTING

 Scissors
 Plastic mesh
 Small foam ball
 Twist-tie
 Liquid tempera paint
 Shallow tray or dish
 Paper

Cut out a square of plastic mesh, large enough to gather around a small foam ball. Secure the ends with a twist-tie. Pour liquid tempera paint into a shallow tray or dish. Dip the mesh ball into the paint, and dab the mesh onto a piece of paper. Use different colours for a unique effect.

SPONGE PRINTING

 Scissors
 Small thick sponges
 Clothespins
 Print pad
 Paper

Cut sponges into various shapes. On the top of each sponge cut two slots for the clothespins to clip into, making the slots about a quarter-inch deep and three-quarter-inches apart. Clip the clothespins to the top of the sponge for handles. Press the sponges onto the print pad and stamp them onto the paper. Use various shapes and colours for an interesting effect.

Sculpting

Sculpting, creating three-dimensional structures, challenges a child's imagination. Not only is it artistic, but messing around with Super Goop and other modeling compounds can also encourage a scientific interest in your child (science begins as a "hands-on" activity).

Many different materials can be used for sculpting. Your child is probably familiar with playdough and modeling clay (see Appendix A). Following are some different ideas you may want to try.

SUPER GOOP

Saucepan
2 cups water
½ cup cornstarch
Food colouring
Mixing spoon
Zippered freezer bags (optional)

Boil water in saucepan. Add cornstarch and stir until smooth. Add food colouring and stir – adjust the amount of food colouring until you get the colour you want. Remove from heat and cool. Let your child squish away on the tabletop, or, for less mess (or younger children) pour the mixture into two zippered freezer bags and seal. Your child can squish the bag or trace letters, numbers, or shapes on the outside of the bag.

WHIPPED SNOW

2 cups warm water
1 cup pure laundry soap or soap flakes
Large bowl
Electric mixer
Food colouring (optional)

Put water and soap in a large bowl and beat with electric mixer until very fluffy. Add colour if desired. If you like, separate the mixture into a number of bowls, and tint each a different colour. Have your child mould the fluff into shapes and allow the shapes to dry.

HOMEMADE SILLY PUTTY

  2 parts white glue
  1 part liquid starch
  Small mixing bowl
  Airtight container

Combine glue and starch in a bowl and mix well. Let dry until the putty is workable. You may have to add a bit more glue or starch. (This may not work well on a humid day.) Experiment! Store in an airtight container.

SUGAR CUBE SCULPTURE

  Sugar cubes
  Glue
  Styrofoam tray, a paper plate, or a piece of heavy cardboard
  Food colouring or liquid tempera paint

Let your child create wonderful sculptures by gluing sugar cubes onto a styrofoam meat tray, paper plate, or piece of heavy cardboard, and also onto each other. You can colour the cubes by quickly dipping them into food colouring, or by lightly dabbing them with liquid tempera paint.

PLASTER HAND & FOOTPRINTS

  Patch plaster or plaster of Paris
  1¼ cups water
  Tin can
  Mixing spoon
  Paper plates
  Picture hook (optional)

To make the plaster mix, stir two cups of patch plaster or plaster of Paris and one and a quarter cups water in a tin can. This mixture should be as thick as pea soup so it can cast without air bubbles. Plaster of Paris dries in about 10 to 20 minutes, while patch plaster takes 20 to 40 minutes to dry.

To make a cast of your child's hand or footprint, pour one inch of plaster mix into a paper plate. Wait two minutes for plaster of Paris, six minutes for patch plaster. Have your child press her hand or foot gently into the plaster. The imprint should not go to the bottom of the plate. Hold for one to two minutes and remove. Let the imprint sit overnight, then peel the plate from the print. If you like, glue a picture hook to the back and hang the print on your child's wall.

Papier Mache

Papier-mâché can be a very messy activity, but is a lot of fun for children and adults alike. Papier-mâché is a special kind of paper modeling that uses paste in combination with paper such as newsprint, paper toweling, gift-wrap, crepe paper, tissue paper, construction paper, or aluminum foil. Paper can be torn into two-inch (or larger) squares or long strips. Torn edges glue better than cut edges and result in a more interesting finished appearance.

For young children, a basic flour-and-water paste is the best bonding material to use. Begin with one cup of water; mix in about a quarter cup of flour until the mixture is thin and runny. Stir this mixture into five cups lightly boiling water. Gently boil and stir for two to three minutes. Cool until you can dip the paper into it.

Pour the paste into a shallow tray. Dip strips of paper into the tray, or brush paste on with a paintbrush. Paste the strips over a form such as an inflated balloon, an empty toilet paper or paper towel roll, or even crumpled newspaper. Add as many layers as you like; model the form with your fingers as you go. Tissue paper can be used as the final layer for a colourful finish.

PAPIER-MACHE HAT

> Papier-mâché paste
> Two large squares of wrapping paper
> String
> Paint

To make a fancy hat, paste together two big squares of wrapping paper with papier-mâché paste. Set this on your child's head, mould the crown of the hat, and tie a string around your child's forehead to hold the shape. After ten minutes, remove the hat, shape, let dry and paint.

PAPIER-MACHE BRACELET

Cardboard tube or baby bottle
Scissors
Papier-mâché paste
Newsprint or other paper
Coloured tissue paper or paint

For this project you will need a cardboard tube large enough in diamater to slip over your child's hand. Cut one- or two-inch pieces of the tube and cover the pieces with layers of paper and paste. Finish with brightly coloured strips of tissue paper or paint. Or, instead of using a cardboard tube, use a bottle with the appropriate diameter (baby bottles work well). Grease or powder the bottle, then start with moulding a layer of newsprint around the bottle. Add a layer of heavier construction paper for strength, then add an additional six layers of papier-mâché. Remove the bracelet from the bottle and finish with paint or strips of tissue paper.

PAPIER-MACHE PINATA

Large inflated balloon
String
Newsprint or other paper
Papier-mâché paste
Small toys and candy
Crepe paper or tissue paper
Paints

This is a great project to make for a birthday party or other special occasion. Hang a big balloon from a string and cover it with many layers of paper and paste, leaving a hole about six inches in diameter at the top of the balloon, around the string. This will take several days to dry. When dry, pop the balloon and pour in toys and candy, then cover the opening with more paper and paste. Let dry again, then decorate the outside with fringed crepe paper or paints. Have the children try to break the piñata by taking turns swinging at it with a toy baseball bat or golf club.

Cutting & Pasting

Most young children gain enormous pleasure from the use of scissors and the feel of paste. Buy your child a good pair of child-safe scissors and teach her how to use them safely. Show her how to keep the edges sharp by cutting sandpaper.

For paste, you can use commercial white glue or make glue or paste using the recipes in Appendix A. Glue and paste is best applied with a small paintbrush, although Popsicle sticks or plastic applicators from the art store can also be used. For variety, tint the glue with food colouring.

Keep a stack of old magazines and catalogues on hand for cutting. An old wallpaper book is also great for all the interesting shapes and patterns it contains. Cut out circles, squares, rectangles, triangles, or other creative shapes and glue them onto construction paper to make designs and pictures.

TISSUE ART

> Glue
> Paper cup or small plastic container
> Water
> Paint brush
> Paper
> Tissue paper cut into ½-by-16-inch strips
> Scissors
> Sequins, beads, glitter (optional)

Pour a small amount of glue into a paper cup or small plastic container and add about a quarter cup water to get the consistency of paint. Have your child use a paintbrush to paint the glue solution onto a piece of paper. Then crumple up strips of brightly coloured tissue paper and press them onto the paper. Use a variety of colours and add sequins, beads, and glitter for a real piece of art.

FUNNY FACE

Old magazines
Scissors
Paper
Glue

Look through old magazines, searching for pictures of faces, and cut out as many eyes, noses, mouths, ears, and heads of hair as you can find. Mix them up and have your child piece together a funny face; then paste it onto a piece of paper.

TORN TISSUE DESIGN

Tissue paper
White glue
Paintbrush
White poster board
Acrylic polymer (optional)
Synthetic paint brush (optional)

Have your child tear various colours of tissue paper into large pieces. Brush white glue thinned with water onto the back of each piece and arrange them on a piece of white poster board. Show your child how to create new colours by overlapping two pieces of different tissue paper; yellow over red makes orange, light blue over pink makes purple, and so on. To give a nice sheen to the finished product, coat it with acrylic polymer using a synthetic paint brush (available at an art supply store).

PERSONAL PUZZLE

Old magazines, catalogues, or greeting cards
Photograph of your child (optional)
Cardboard
Glue
Scissors

Cut out pictures from magazines, catalogues, or greeting cards, or use an enlarged photograph of your child. Glue the picture onto a piece of cardboard that has been cut the same size. When dry, let your child cut the picture into pieces to create her own puzzle. Puzzles are great for helping your child recognize shapes – a prerequisite to learning letters and numbers.

CHINESE LANTERN

> Construction paper
> Scissors
> Glue or stapler

Fold construction paper in half lengthwise and show your child how to cut from the folded edge to within one and a half inches of the opposite side. When cuts have been made along the entire length of the paper, unfold and form into a cylinder by joining together the short uncut ends of paper. Glue or staple another strip of construction paper for a handle.

PICTURE PLACE MAT

> Family photographs
> Cardboard or construction paper
> Glue
> Clear contact paper

Give your child the family photographs that didn't make it into your photo album. Have her glue them onto a piece of cardboard or construction paper and cover with clear contact paper. This makes a great gift for Daddy, grandparents, and other family members.

CIRCLE BEAR

> Brown and white construction paper
> Scissors
> Glue
> Black marker or crayon

Cut circles of brown construction paper. You will need one large circle for the body, two small circles for paws, a medium circle for the head, two half circles for feet, and two half circles for ears. Show your child how to glue them onto white construction paper to form a bear. Your child can use a black marker or crayon to draw a face. You can also cut out small, white circles to glue into place on the paws, ears, and tummy.

GINGERBREAD PEOPLE

    Thin cardboard or brown construction paper
    Pen or marker
    Scissors
    Glue
    Lace, ribbon, fabric scraps
    Pieces of cereal, small candy, or licorice

Draw the outline of a gingerbread girl or boy on thin cardboard or brown construction paper. Your child can cut it out and dress it by gluing bits of lace and ribbon or scraps of fabric onto the figure. Make a face out of cereal or candy.

SHADOW SILHOUETTE

    Bright light
    Construction paper
    Tape
    Pencil
    Scissors
    Glue

Have your child stand sideways against a wall and shine a bright light on her to make a profile shadow on the wall. Tape a piece of construction paper onto the wall shadow and trace your child's silhouette. Have her cut it out and mount it on another piece of construction paper in a contrasting colour.

JELLY BEAN PICTURE

    Cardboard or paper plate
    Glue
    Jelly beans

Help your child draw a picture with glue on a piece of cardboard or paper plate. Have her place jelly beans on the glue. You can give this a seasonal theme by using pastel jelly beans on a rabbit picture for Easter, or green jelly beans on a Christmas tree and beans of other colours for lights and decorations. Warn your child not to eat jelly beans that have glue on them, or better yet, use edible Ornamental Frosting (see Appendix A) instead of glue.

TISSUE PAPER MIRROR

> Cardboard
> Scissors
> Aluminum foil
> Glue
> Tissue paper cut into 4-inch squares

Cut cardboard into the shape of a hand mirror. Cut a piece of aluminum foil into a corresponding shape and glue it onto one side of the cardboard to make "glass". Have your child crumple four-inch squares of coloured tissue paper into balls and glue them close together on the other side of the mirror to make a flower-covered back.

FOIL WRAPPING PAPER

> Heavy-duty aluminum foil
> Coloured tissue paper
> Acrylic polymer
> Water
> Synthetic paint brush

Make your own foil wrapping paper using heavy-duty aluminum foil, tissue paper and acrylic polymer (available at art supply stores). Tear or cut pieces of tissue paper and arrange them on the aluminum foil. Mix the acrylic polymer with a little water and brush over the tissue paper, letting it soak through. It will make the paper stick to the foil and give it a really glossy finish.

EGGSHELL MOSAIC

This is a great way to use up the remains of the Easter eggs. Your child will have a lot of fun breaking up all the eggshells, and the pretty colours make a great mosaic.

> Coloured eggshells
> Construction paper
> Crayon, pen, or marker
> Glue

On a piece of construction paper, have your child draw a simple design. Fill it in with glue and add the bits of coloured eggshell. If you don't have coloured eggshells available, dye your eggshells just as you would dye hard-boiled eggs (see Chapter 9).

FAVOURITE FOODS

> Old magazines
> Scissors
> Glue
> Paper plate
> Pipe cleaner
> Tape

Have your child cut pictures of her favourite foods from old magazines. Paste them onto a paper plate; tape a curved pipe cleaner onto the back for hanging. Or make a place mat by gluing the pictures onto a piece of construction paper and covering with clear contact paper.

Crafts & other fun Things to Make

Not only will craft projects challenge your child's imagination and artistic ability, they will fill in many hours of a rainy afternoon and help keep your child stimulated and happy. Make crafts as gifts for friends and family, or use them to brighten up your child's room and the rest of the house. Most of these projects can be made using objects found around the house or collected on your daily walks.

COOKIE CUTTER CARDS

Construction paper
Crayon, pen, or marker
Scraps of fabric or lace, paper doilies, glitter, stickers, and so on

Fold a piece of plain or construction paper in half to make a greeting card. Have your child trace around cookie cutters in appropriate shapes, e.g., hearts for Valentines, trees or angels for Christmas. The card can then be decorated with scraps of fabric or lace, paper doilies, glitter, stickers, and so on.

STYROFOAM PEOPLE

Styrofoam balls and blocks in different sizes
Toothpicks
Scraps of yarn and fabric
Glue
Markers or paint

Use toothpicks to join the Styrofoam shapes together to form people, a snowman, animals, and so on. Glue scraps of yarn and fabric onto the Styrofoam to make hair and clothes. Use markers or paint to add faces or other details.

PLAYDOUGH JEWELRY

Playdough
Toothpick or large, blunt needle
Clear gloss enamel or nail polish
String

Have your child roll small pieces of playdough into balls to make beads. Pierce each bead with a toothpick or large blunt needle and allow to dry for several days. Check holes after a day to see if they need repunching. When dry, coat with clear gloss enamel or clear nail polish to bring out the colour. Thread beads onto a string and knot the ends together to create a necklace or bracelet.

HOMEMADE FAN

Paper
Crayons or markers

Have your child draw a design on a piece of construction paper or plain paper and show her how to make a fan by folding the paper back and forth in one-inch folds. She can colour one or both sides of the fan. As a variation, fold the fan first, then unfold and have your child colour and decorate each panel separately.

SPOON PEOPLE

Wooden kitchen spoon
Glue
Yarn
Buttons
Marker

Use a wooden kitchen spoon to make a spoon person. Have your child glue yarn onto the top of the spoon to make hair and buttons to make eyes. Draw a mouth and nose with markers. Make several of these for a spoon family, and encourage your child to tell a story with these little people.

PAPER TOWEL ART

A quicker, cleaner alternative to "real" painting.

Paper towel
Newspaper
Food colouring, or unsweetened Kool-Aid or Jell-O jelly powder
Clean, empty salt shakers (optional)

Lay a piece of paper towel over newspaper and show your child how to drop food colouring onto the paper towel. Use different colours to make an interesting design. For variety, wet the paper towel first and lightly shake unsweetened Kool-Aid drink mix or Jell-O powder onto it. Use a variety of vivid colours and let them dry for a beautiful result. For younger children who might be tempted to dump the entire package at once, put the drink mix or Jell-O powder in a clean, empty salt shaker before using.

COFFEE CAN CANISTERS

Empty coffee cans
Paintings, drawings, or other artwork your child has made
Scissors
Glue
Clear contact paper

Use your child's artwork to create some decorative and useful canisters out of empty coffee cans. Cut the artwork to completely cover the can and glue it on, overlapping the edges. To protect the artwork, cover the outside of the can with clear contact paper. These canisters are great for holding crayons, playdough, cookie cutters, or small toys, and they make fun alternatives to gift-wrap.

BINOCULARS

This idea may sound a bit ridiculous, but you will be amazed at how much fun a child will have with these!

Two toilet paper rolls
Tape
Markers, crayons, stickers, and so on

Tape two toilet paper rolls together to make a pair of binoculars for your child. She can decorate them with markers, stickers, and so on, and use them to spot interesting things as you go for a walk or ride in the car.

RAINBOW FAN

Paint sample cards
Hole punch
Paper fastener
Yarn or string

Pick up some colourful paint sample cards from your local hardware store. Punch a hole in the centre of the bottom and top of each card. At one end, join the cards with a paper fastener. At the other, lace yarn through the holes in each card to form the top of a fan.

WAX PAPER ART

Newspaper
Wax paper
Crayons
Grater or knife
Hot iron

Place several layers of newspaper on your work surface. Place a sheet of wax paper on top of the newspaper, wax side up. Shave, chop finely, or grate crayons onto the wax paper. Place a second sheet of wax paper, wax side down, on top of the first sheet (so that crayon pieces are between). Cover with several layers of newspaper and iron with a hot iron until crayons are melted. Hang to dry.

FRAMED FLOWERS

Flowers or leaves
Crayon shavings
Wax paper
Newspaper
Iron

Go out on a walk with your child and pick some pretty spring flowers or fall leaves. At home, make shavings of brightly coloured crayons with a grater or knife. Place a piece of wax paper, wax side up, on top of several layers of newspaper on your work surface. Arrange the flowers or leaves on top of the wax paper and sprinkle with crayon shavings. Cover with another piece of wax paper, wax side down. Place several layers of newspaper on top and iron thoroughly until the crayons are melted. Hang to dry. A smaller version glued to one half of a folded piece of construction paper makes a unique and beautiful greeting card.

WAXED LEAVES

Leaves
Newspaper
Wax paper
Iron

On a fall walk with your child, collect a variety of types and colours of leaves. At home, cover your ironing board with several layers of newspaper, then place a sheet of wax paper on top. Have your child arrange her leaves on top of the wax paper. Place a second sheet of wax paper over the leaves. Cover with a layer of newspaper and place a medium-hot iron on top. Hold the iron in place for about 30 seconds. Then move the iron to another section of the wax paper. Continue until all areas of the wax paper have been heated. Lift off the paper and remove the leaves. They should be waxed enough to retain their shape. Arrange them in a vase or use them in some other art work.

PASTA PICTURE

> Pasta in various shapes
> Paper plate or piece of cardboard
> Glue
> Tempera paints
> Paintbrush

Glue various shapes of pasta onto a paper plate or a piece of cardboard, and paint the pasta with tempera paints. If you prefer, dye the pasta ahead of time by mixing half a cup of alcohol with food colouring. The larger the pasta, the longer it will take to absorb the colour. Dry the pasta on newspaper covered with wax paper. When the pasta is dry, use it to create a pasta picture.

PARTY HATS

> Construction paper
> Crayons, markers, stickers, and other decorative items
> Tape or stapler
> Scissors
> Elastic thread or ribbon

Let your child decorate a piece of construction paper with crayons, markers, stickers, and so on. Fold the paper into a cone shape, tape or staple the overlapping edges together, and cut the bottom edge so it is even. Staple a length of elastic thread or ribbon to each side for hat straps.

PAPER BAG KITE

Large paper bag
Hole punch
Paper ring reinforcements
Scissors
String
Paint or markers
Stapler or glue
Crepe paper streamers

Punch a hole in each of the four corners of a large paper bag, at least one inch from the edge of the bag. Place a paper ring reinforcement on each hole. Cut two three-foot lengths of string and tie each end into a hole to form two loops. Cut another three-foot length of string and tie it through the two loops to create a handle. Have your child decorate the bag with paint or markers, and give her crepe paper streamers to glue or staple onto the bag. When your child holds onto the string and runs, the kite will fill with air and float behind her.

EGG CARTON BUTTERFLY

Cardboard egg carton
Scissors
Tempera paint
Paintbrush
Pipe cleaners
Construction paper
Markers
Stapler

Cut the sectioned portion of an egg carton in half lengthwise so that you have a strip with six cups on it. Turn the strip upside down and paint with tempera paint. Attach pipe cleaners to the head for feelers. Cut wings from construction paper and decorate with paint or markers; staple to the side of the carton. Use your imagination to make variations; for example, use one cup of the carton to make a turtle or ladybug; use three cups to make a bumblebee; or use a full half carton to make a caterpillar.

PINWHEEL

Plain or construction paper
Crayons, markers, glitter, stickers, and other decorative items
Scissors
Tape
Paper fastener
Cardboard cut into a small circle
Straw, wooden dowel, or unsharpened pencil

Have your child decorate a square piece of paper with crayons, markers, paint, glitter, stickers, and so on. Mark the centre of the square and cut from each corner into the centre, stopping one inch from the centre. Fold every other point into the centre and tape; make sure the decorated side of the paper is on the outside. Push a paper fastener through a small circular piece of cardboard, then through the centre of the pinwheel. Fasten around a straw, wooden dowel, or unsharpened pencil.

NOODLE NECKLACE

Macaroni noodles
String
Tempera paint
Paintbrush

Make a noodle necklace by threading macaroni noodles on a string. Knot the ends together and paint with tempera paints. Let the necklace dry thoroughly before letting your child wear her creation.

NAPKIN RINGS

Empty paper towel or toilet paper rolls
Scissors
Crayons, paints, stickers, or glitter

Make napkin rings for a special occasion or to give as a gift. Cut empty paper towel or toilet paper rolls into one-and-a-half-inch pieces. Have your child decorate them with crayons, paints, stickers, or glitter.

MODERN ART

Piece of cardboard or paper plate
Glue or paste
Small household items (cereal, buttons, macaroni, sequins, cut-up
straws, plastic jug lids, and so on)

Give your child a strong piece of cardboard or a paper plate, some glue, and small items of different sizes, shapes and textures: cereal, buttons, macaroni, sequins, cut-up straws, plastic juice jug lids, and so on. Let your child create her own version of modern art.

EGG CARTON FLOWERS

Empty egg cartons
Scissors
Paint, markers, or crayons
Pipe cleaner
Green construction paper
Glue

Cut apart an egg carton into individual sections and have your child paint the sections with a variety of colours. (Markers or crayons can also be used.) Poke a pipe cleaner through the bottom of each section to make a stem. Cut leaf shapes out of green construction paper and glue onto the pipe cleaner. Several colourful flowers in a bud vase make a great gift or a decorative table centrepiece.

PAPER DOLL CHAIN

Large sheets of paper or newspaper
Scissors
Crayons or markers

Fold a large sheet of paper like a fan (newspaper, a cut-open paper bag, or computer paper works well). The fan folds should be as wide as you want your dolls to be. Draw a doll shape with arms and legs extended away from the body, so that the hands and feet fall on the folds. Cut out the doll shape, taking care not to cut the folds at the hands and feet; if you cut through, you will end up with a lot of single paper dolls instead of a chain. Unfold the chain and let your child decorate each doll with crayons or markers. With a little practice, your child will soon be able to make a doll chain on her own.

PICTURE SOAP

> Bar of soap
> Glue
> Photograph or other picture
> Canning wax
> Small empty can
> Pan
> Hot water
> Paintbrush

Glue a photograph or any other picture onto a bar of soap. Melt canning wax in a small empty can in a pan of hot water. To waterproof the picture, dip a paintbrush in the melted wax and paint it over the picture. Your child can take a bath with her special soap or save it to give as a gift.

STRAW HOLDERS

This is a good idea for place cards for a birthday or other occasion.

> Thin cardboard
> Scissors
> Hole punch
> Crayons, markers, or stickers
> Straws

This is a great project for a special occasion or holiday, or just to make any day special. Use thin cardboard (a paper plate or file folder works well) to cut out a square, circle, or special shape (like a heart for Valentine's Day). Use a hole punch to make a hole at the top and bottom of your cutout, then have your child decorate the cutout with crayons, markers, or stickers. Insert a drinking straw into one hole and out the other. Your child can then use this to drink her favourite beverage.

FEATHER HEADBAND

    Construction paper or poster board
    Scissors
    Stapler
    Glue
    Feathers (optional)
    Markers or crayons (optional)

Cut a strip of brown construction paper or poster board about one and a half inches wide. Measure the length by placing the headband around your child's head and stapling the ends together to fit snugly. Cut several feather shapes out of coloured construction paper (or gather some real feathers on a walk) and glue to the headband. Your child can draw a design on the headband with markers or crayons if she wishes.

PICTURE FRAME

    Baby food or other jar lid, or metal lid from frozen juice cans
    Photograph
    Pen
    Scissors
    Glue
    Ribbon
    Magnets

Place a jar lid or the metal lid from a frozen juice can on the photograph you wish to frame and trace around it. Cut out the photo and glue it inside the lid. If you use a jar lid, tie a ribbon around the outside of the lid. Glue a magnet to the back of the lid and place it on the refrigerator.

PARADE SHAKER

    Paper towel or toilet paper roll
    Stapler
    Crepe paper
    Scissors

Decorate an empty paper towel or toilet paper roll by stapling several twelve-inch strips of crepe paper to each end of the roll. Cut each strip into thirds, lengthwise, to make each strip into three narrow strips. Scrunch each strip with your fingers to make the shaker look fuller. Let your little one have her own parade by holding onto the roll and shaking the streamer. If you use toilet paper rolls, attach the streamers to only one end, so your child has plenty of room to hold onto the shaker.

TALL TREES

Newspaper
Tape
Scissors
Empty toilet paper or paper towel roll
Piece of heavy cardboard

Roll up the long side of one sheet of newspaper and tape it closed. Cut one end of the roll into a fringe using long snips, fairly close together. Reach inside the fringed end of the roll and carefully pull out the centre to make the tree spiral up until it's tall. The fringes become the leaves of the tree; curl them or dress them up with paper flowers. To display your tree, stand it in an empty toilet paper or paper towel roll taped to a heavy cardboard base.

BIRD FEEDER

Pine cone
String
Peanut butter
Knife for spreading
Bird seed

Make your own bird feeder with peanut butter, a pine cone, and bird seed. Tie a string around the top of the pine cone under the ridges, so the string stays in place, and knot it, leaving enough string for hanging. Thoroughly cover the pine cone with peanut butter, then roll it in bird seed. Hang the feeder outside near a window and your child can watch the birds eat.

TOY BOAT

  Styrofoam meat tray
  Straw
  White construction paper
  Scissors
  Tape

Make a toy sailboat with a clean Styrofoam meat tray. Insert a straw into the tray for the mast. Cut a triangular sail from white construction paper and tape to the straw. Your child can sail her boat in the bathtub, a swimming pool, or a tub of water.

ROCK ART

  Rocks
  Glue
  Paint
  Paintbrush
  Playdough or fabric scraps, ribbon, or lace

Make rock people or rock animals by gluing together rocks you have collected on walks. Your child can then paint her rock art and add accessories made out of playdough or fabric scraps, ribbon, or lace.

COAT RACK

  Four eight-penny nails
  1-foot length of 1-by-2-inch wood
  Hammer
  Tempera paint, markers, or crayons

This is something your child can make that is useful, and it makes a good gift for someone special. Show your child how to hammer a row of four eight-penny nails into a one-foot length of one-by-two-inch wood. The wood can then be painted with tempera paints, markers, or crayons. Be sure to display this in a prominent place.

PAPER BAG VEST

Large brown paper bag
Scissors
Paint

Make a vest from a brown paper bag by cutting a head hole, arm holes, and a fringe along the bottom. Your child can paint and decorate the vest. When the vest is dry, your child can wear it.

CHAPTER NINE

Holiday Activities

*The first holiday may have been invented to celebrate fertility or planting or har-
vest, but we're sure a mother was behind it. Even then she must have known that
nothing could cure her day-to-day drudgery as well as a holiday or brighten the
eye of a small child so quickly.*

MARGUERITE KELLY AND ELIA PARSONS

NOTHING CAN DISRUPT YOUR DAILY ROUTINE LIKE A HOLIDAY, YET
nothing is quite so important. Mothers and small children alike often
need the lift of a special day on which we can focus energy and attention.
In addition to celebrating birthdays and traditional holidays, make the
most of each small victory and accomplishment. You don't have to go all
out all the time; put a candle on the dinner table and use your best china
to make even an ordinary day extraordinary. Most of the fun and excitement comes from the anticipation that builds as the celebration draws
near, so be sure to allow your child to take part in the planning and
preparation for each festivity.

Birthday Celebrations

For the first few years of your child's life, a family dinner complete with
birthday cake and candles is usually sufficient for a birthday celebration.
But somewhere around the third or fourth year, your child will probably
want to invite a few friends over for a "real" birthday party. This will usu-

ally be about two hours long and consist mainly of eating and opening gifts. Keep the food simple; sandwiches, pizza, hotdogs, carrot sticks, fruit, juice, and chocolate milk are some suggestions. Older children will enjoy a few simple games, such as London Bridge, Pin the Tail on the Donkey, Follow the Leader, Red Light/Green Light, or Simon Says. If you really want to go all out and organize a theme party for your child, there are many excellent birthday party books available in bookstores or at your local library.

If you find the commercialism of even a small child's party appalling, you may want to consider asking parents to spend not more than a few dollars on a present. You can also be good to the environment and avoid spending a small fortune on matching hats, plates, cups, napkins, and tablecloth by using brightly coloured linen and unbreakable plates. Have each child make his own party hat with construction paper, markers, stickers and glitter (see Chapter 8) and substitute a small, wrapped gift for each child in place of a goodie bag (or dispense with this custom altogether). Store-bought thank-you notes for gifts received can be replaced with your child's original artwork.

BIRTHDAY TIME CAPSULE

Envelope
Writing paper
Pen

This is a wonderful tradition for young and old alike. Each birthday person prepares information to be put into their "time capsule". Ask questions of young children and write down their responses. You may want to ask about favourite foods, songs, activities, friends, and so on. Ask what your child looks forward to over the year, and what he expects life to be like next year on his birthday. When everything is written down, place the paper in an envelope and mark the birthday person's name on it and the Date to be Opened (next year on his birthday). You'll all have a lot of fun when the time capsule is opened.

VIDEO TIME CAPSULE

Video camera
Video tape

If you have access to a video camera, consider taping your Birthday Time Capsule instead of writing it down. Ask questions of younger children. Older children may enjoy just talking about themselves and their day-to-day life. Once the time capsule is taped, put the tape away and don't watch it until the following year on your child's birthday. If doing this for more than one child, use a different tape for each. Add a new segment each year, keeping the previous ones, as well. Over the years, you will be able to watch your child grow up on his time capsule tape.

SUPER CHOCOLATE BIRTHDAY CAKE

This chocolate cake is quick and easy to make, and it is absolutely delicious. After the cake is baked and cooled, insert foil-wrapped coins into one of the layers before frosting. When cutting the cake, be sure each child receives a piece with a coin in it. You may not want to include coins in a cake for very young children because of the danger of choking.

2 cups white sugar
6 Tbsp. butter
2 eggs, beaten
1 cup cocoa
Boiling water
1 tsp. soda
1 cup boiling water
2 cups flour
2 tsp. baking powder

Preheat the oven to 350 degrees. Cream sugar and butter; add beaten egg. Add enough boiling water to the cocoa to make two cups of liquid. Add the cocoa liquid to the sugar mixture. Mix soda and one cup boiling water, and add to the sugar/cocoa mixture. Add flour and baking powder, mix well, and pour into two greased 8-inch or 9-inch layer cake pans. Bake for 30 minutes.

FUDGY CHOCOLATE FROSTING

This recipe frosts one two-layer 8-inch or 9-inch cake.

> 3 Tbsp. butter, melted
> ¼ cup cocoa
> ¼ cup milk
> ½ tsp. vanilla
> 2 cups icing sugar, sifted

Combine melted butter with cocoa. Blend in milk, vanilla, and sifted icing sugar until smooth.

New Year's Day

The beginning of a new year is a time for a fresh start, a time for new beginnings. Whether you celebrate with a traditional family dinner or eat take-out Chinese food, the arrival of a new year is indeed an occasion worth celebrating.

New Year's Day is often the time we assess ourselves and set goals for our future. Consider adapting the Birthday Time Capsule or Video Time Capsule ideas (see Birthday Celebrations) for New Year's. Tape- or video-record or write down each family member's resolutions and hopes for the new year to begin a New Year's tradition that you and your child will cherish for years to come.

FRIENDS FAR & NEAR

> Christmas cards you have received
> Basket

After Christmas is over, place the Christmas cards you received into a basket and set it on your table. Starting in January, take one card out of the basket each day and talk about that person or family with your child. If prayers are a part of your child's bedtime routine, this is a good way to include someone special each night.

Valentine's Day

Valentine's Day is the day for celebrating love. Start your preparations several weeks in advance as you make heart-shaped cookies, cards, and valentine crafts. On February 14th, dress the whole family in red and put your heart-shaped cookie cutter to work for toast, sandwiches, apples, cheese, and Finger Jell-O (see Chapter 3). A small Valentine's party can be a simple and fun way to celebrate this special day.

HEART PEOPLE

> Construction paper in red, white, and pink
> Pencil
> Scissors
> Glue or paste

Using red, white, and pink construction paper, trace and cut hearts ranging in size from two to six inches. Glue the hearts together in different combinations to form heart people, using large hearts for heads and bodies, smaller ones for arms and legs. You can also try making heart animals.

HEART NECKLACE

> Plain or construction paper
> Scissors
> Liquid tempera paint
> Hole punch
> Yarn
> Photo of your child (optional)
> Glue (optional)

Cut a heart shape as large as your child's hand out of plain or construction paper. Dip his hand in liquid tempera paint and press it on the paper. When the paint is dry, punch a hole in the top of the heart and string yarn through it to make a necklace. Write a valentine's message on it, and glue a picture of your child on the other side, if you wish. Send or give the heart necklace to a special friend or relative.

VALENTINE MOBILE

> Valentines your child has received
> Hole punch
> Thread or yarn
> Coat hanger

Have your child punch holes in his valentines, thread them onto a piece of thread or yarn, and hang them from a coat hanger to create a mobile. Hang the finished mobile from a curtain rod.

VALENTINE PLACE MAT

> Valentines your child has received
> Construction paper or light cardboard
> Glue or paste
> Clear contact paper

Have your child glue his favourite valentines onto a large piece of construction paper or light cardboard. Cover this collage with clear contact paper to make a place mat.

HEART WINDOW DECORATING

> Plain or construction paper
> Scissors
> Can of spray-on artificial snow

Fold several pieces of paper in half and cut out heart shapes in varying sizes. The pieces of paper out of which the hearts have been cut will serve as stencils. Tape them to the window in an interesting arrangement and spray with artificial snow. Remove the stencils to see the heart shapes on the window.

VALENTINE CHAIN

> Construction paper in red, white, and pink
> Scissors
> Glue or paste

Cut strips of red, white, and pink construction paper, three to four inches long and one-half to one inch wide. Give the strips to your child and have him form a circle with one strip, gluing the ends together. Take the next strip and loop it through the first circle, again gluing the ends together. Tell your child to make a chain as long as he wants. Use it to decorate doorways, walls, and so on.

LACED HEART

> Poster board or heavy construction paper in valentine colours
>   (white, pink, red, purple)
> Hole punch
> Tape
> Ribbon in contrasting colours
> Photo of your child (optional)
> Glue (optional)
> Magnet (optional)

Cut a large heart shape out of poster board or heavy construction paper. Punch an even number of holes around the outside edge of the heart. Wrap tape around one end of a ribbon to make threading easier. Show your child how to weave the ribbon through the holes, starting at either the bottom or top of the heart. Tie the ends in a bow. Help your child write a valentine's message on the heart. If you like, glue a photo of your child to the front of the heart and a magnet to the back.

St. Patrick's Day

Whether or not St. Patrick's Day is a big deal in your family, a holiday such as this can help break up the monotony of the last days of winter. Dress in green and invite a few friends over for a small St. Patrick's Day celebration. Make Green Hats together and play a few simple games. Serve green Finger Jell-O (see Chapter 3) and cupcakes or sugar cookies with green icing (or decorate them as a party activity). Colour white grape juice green with a drop or two of food colouring, or serve limeade or green Kool-Aid. Wind up the day with your own St. Patrick's Day parade wearing the hats you have made and marching to the beat of a Coffee Can Drum, Pie Plate Tambourine (see Chapter 7), or other homemade rhythm instruments.

GREEN HATS

Green paint
16-by-20-inch sheets of newspaper
1-by-2-inch piece of sponge
Shallow dish or plastic lids (for paint)

Fold sheets of newspaper in half, short end to short end. Fold the top corners (folded end) over so that they meet in the centre. Fold up the bottom edges so they meet the folded over edges. Pour a small amount of paint in a shallow dish or plastic lid, dip the sponge in the paint, and let your child decorate the hat.

HIDE THE SHAMROCK

While this game works best with a few children, you can still play it when there's just the two of you.

Green construction paper
Scissors

Cut a shamrock out of green construction paper. Choose a child to be "it". While other children hide their eyes, "it" hides the shamrock within a designated area. Everyone then opens their eyes and tries to find the shamrock. The finder gets to be "it" for the next round.

Easter

Easter is the traditional Christian holiday that celebrates the resurrection of Jesus Christ. It is also a time to celebrate the coming of spring and all the joyous signs of new life. Consider holding a small Easter party for your child and a few friends. Make some Easter Bunny Ears and decorate eggs with your guests. Have an informal Easter parade with decorated wagons and tricycles. An Easter egg or candy hunt can be held either indoors or out, depending on the weather. Remember that children enjoy the planning and anticipation, so start your Easter crafts and activities early.

PAPER PLATE EASTER BUNNY

Large paper plate
Small paper plate
Glue
Scissors
Pink construction paper
Stapler
Crayons or markers
Cotton ball

Glue a small paper plate to a large paper plate to form the head and body of the bunny. Cut out bunny ears from pink construction paper and glue or staple to the head. Draw the bunny face with crayons or markers, and glue a cotton ball on the back for the tail.

PAPIER-MACHE EASTER EGG

Papier-mâché paste
Shallow dish
Balloon
Tape
1" torn strips of newspaper or paper towel
Pie tin
Paint
Paintbrushes
Coloured tissue paper (optional)
Shellac

Mix up some papier-mâché paste (see Appendix A) and put it in a shallow dish. Inflate a balloon and tape it to the top of the table. Dip strips of newspaper in the paste and place them on the balloon, overlapping edges slightly. Cover the balloon completely and let dry. Have your child decorate the covered balloon by painting an Easter egg design, or cover the balloon egg with a layer of tissue paper in pastel Easter colours. Finish with shellac for a shiny, glazed effect.

EASTER GRASS

Store-bought, plastic Easter "grass" is much in abundance at this time of year, but why not grow some real grass in which to hide your Easter eggs?

    Large Easter basket
    Pan, large enough to hold the basket
    Wheat seeds (about 1 lb.)
    Vermiculite (about 1 lb.)
    Plastic wrap

Grow a miniature meadow right in your own Easter basket. About a week before Easter, line a large Easter basket with plastic wrap and fill with vermiculite up to two inches below the rim. Sprinkle the wheat seeds on top of the vermiculite, set the basket in the sink, and add water until the seed bed is moist. You won't have to water it again before Easter. Set the basket in a pan and place in filtered sunlight. Cover loosely with plastic wrap to keep moist; remove the plastic after two days. The wheat will begin to sprout during the next few days, and by Easter morning, you will have real Easter grass for hiding your Easter eggs.

EASTER BUNNY MASK

    Paper plate
    Scissors
    Pink construction paper
    Glue
    Pink or white pipe cleaners
    Yarn
    Hole punch

Turn a paper plate into a bunny mask. Hold the plate against your child's face and mark where the eyes and nose holes should be. Cut out the holes for the eyes and nose. Cut out bunny ears from pink construction paper and glue to the plate. Use pipe cleaners for whiskers. Punch a hole on each side of the plate, and attach two pieces of yarn on either side to tie the mask onto your little bunny's head.

EASTER BUNNY EARS

This is a quick, clean, and very cute craft for even the youngest of Easter bunnies to make. Don't forget to take a picture when you're done!

> Construction paper in white and pink
> Scissors
> Glue
> Stapler

Use white and pink construction paper to cut out bunny-ear shapes, two white and two pink, the pink being slightly smaller. Glue the pink ears onto the white ears. Glue the ears onto a long strip of construction paper, measure to fit your child's head, and staple the ends together to form a headband.

Egg Decorating

There are many different ways to decorate an Easter egg without using commercially prepared egg dyes. You can make your own dye with food colouring or vegetables, or you can make pretty eggs using crayons, paint, fabric, yarn, seeds, and other materials to create different effects.

If you are using hard-boiled eggs, keep them refrigerated. Do not eat them if they are not refrigerated or have been sprayed with acrylic. If you are creating special works of art, you should use blown eggs instead of hard-boiled. Blown eggs are more fragile, and probably not a good idea for really young children, but you can keep them from year to year.

To blow an egg, poke a small hole at each end of the egg with a large needle. Push the needle inside the egg and twist until the yoke is broken. Hold the egg over a bowl and blow hard through the hole at the top until the shell is empty. Rinse the eggshells well and allow to dry completely before decorating. (Save the raw eggs and scramble them for breakfast, or do some baking with your child.)

Once you get going, you'll come up with your own ideas. Here are just a few to get you started.

NATURAL EGG DYE

Sauce pans (one for each colour)
Water, ½ cup for each saucepan
Various food and plant items
Strainer
Hard-boiled or blown eggs
Slotted spoon
Cooking oil
Soft cloth

Pour half a cup of water into each saucepan and add cut-up fruit, vegetables, or plants (try carrots, blueberries, grass, and coffee). Bring to a boil and simmer until the water turns the colour you want. Remove from heat and strain; reserve the water. When the water cools, add eggs and allow to sit in the water until they turn the desired colour. Remove with a slotted spoon and allow to air dry. Polish dry eggs with a small amount of cooking oil and a soft cloth.

FOOD COLOURING EGG DYE

Small bowls or cups, one for each colour
Food colouring, ¼ tsp. for each colour
Hot water, ¾ cup for each colour
White vinegar, 1 Tbsp. for each colour
Hard-boiled or blown eggs
Slotted spoon
Cooking oil
Soft cloth

For each colour, measure a quarter teaspoon of food colouring into a small bowl or cup. Add three-quarter cup hot water and one tablespoon white vinegar to each colour. Add eggs and allow to sit in the water until they turn the desired colour. Remove with a slotted spoon and allow to air dry. Polish dry eggs with a small amount of cooking oil and a soft cloth.

MARBLE EGGS

Grater
Wax paper or newspaper
Crayon stubs
Large glass jar
Hot water
Hard-boiled or blown eggs
Slotted spoon
Empty egg carton
Clear acrylic spray (optional)

Grate peeled crayon stubs over wax paper or newspaper. Fill a large glass jar with very hot water. Drop pinches of grated crayon into the water and add an egg as soon as the crayon begins to melt. Twirl the egg in the water with a slotted spoon; the wax will make a design on the egg. Carefully remove the egg from the water with a slotted spoon and set it in an upside-down egg carton to dry. Spray with clear acrylic when the wax is dry, if desired.

SPONGE PAINTED EGGS

Newspaper
Hard-boiled or blown eggs
Egg cups
Liquid tempera paint
Paper cups or small paint containers (one for each colour)
Small pieces of sponge or foam
Spring-type clothespins (one for each colour)
Clear acrylic spray (optional)

Cover your work surface with newspaper. Place eggs in egg cups. Partially fill paper cups or small paint containers with liquid tempera paint. Clip pieces of sponge to clothespins and dip them into the paint, using the clothespin as handles. Lightly dab the sponges over the top half of the egg and let dry. Turn the eggs over and repeat. Let the eggs dry completely. If you use blown eggs, spray with clear acrylic for a permanent finish.

DIP & DYE EGGS

Hard-boiled eggs
Masking tape
Egg dyes in a variety of colours
Slotted spoon
Cooking oil
Soft cloth

Stick a pattern of masking tape on a hard-boiled egg. Dip them in a natural or commercial egg dye and leave them until they reach the desired colour. Remove the eggs with a slotted spoon and allow to air dry. Remove the masking tape when the eggs are completely dry. Leave the masked areas white, or dip the egg again in a lighter dye. Polish the finished eggs with a small amount of cooking oil and a soft cloth.

WAXED EGGS

Hard-boiled eggs
Wax crayons
Egg dyes in a variety of colours
Slotted spoon
Paper towel
Cooking oil
Soft cloth

Draw a heavy crayon pattern on hard-boiled eggs and dip them in a natural or commercial egg dye in a dark colour. Leave them in until they reach the desired colour. Remove eggs with a slotted spoon and place them in a 200-degree oven for a few minutes to melt the crayon. Wipe with a paper towel and dip again in a lighter colour to fill in the pattern drawn with the crayon. Polish the finished eggs with a small amount of cooking oil and a soft cloth.

CREPE PAPER EGG DYE

Crepe paper, variety of colors
Hot water
Small bowls or cups, one for each colour
Hard-boiled or blown eggs

Slotted spoon
Cooking oil
Soft cloth

Soak crepe paper in hot water in a small bowl or cup, one colour of crepe paper per container. Add eggs and allow to sit in the water until they turn the desired colour. Remove with a slotted spoon and allow to air dry. Polish dry eggs with a small amount of cooking oil and a soft cloth.

Canada Day

Canada Day on July 1st celebrates the anniversary of Confederation in 1867, and so this holiday is Canada's birthday. Whether you celebrate with a patriotic parade or a picnic at the park, a day at the beach or a traditional family barbecue, be sure your child knows why the nation celebrates this day. Fly the flag proudly, decorate and dress with a red and white theme, bake a birthday cake and sing "Happy Birthday, Canada." Your family's Canada Day traditions and celebrations can help your children feel proud of their country.

Use your imagination to adapt some of the activities in this book for your Canada Day celebrations. Make a birthday card for Canada. Bake sugar cookies or cupcakes and decorate them with white icing and red maple leafs. Join layers of strawberry Jell-O with whipped cream to make red and white Finger Jell-O (see Chapter 3). Make a fireworks painting (see Air Painting, Chapter 8). Sing Canadian folk songs and march around your house or yard with a homemade drum. Have fun!

RED AND WHITE SALAD

This one your child will need very little help with.

Strawberries
Bananas

Wash and hull strawberries, and peel and slice bananas. Mix ingredients and serve.

CANADIAN FLAG

As you work to make this Canadian flag, talk with your child about what the colours and shapes represent. Red and white are Canada's official colours as appointed by King George V in 1921. The maple leaf has been associated with Canada since the 1700s, appearing on military badges, decorations, provincial coats of arms, and Canadian coins.

> Red construction paper
> Scissors
> Glue
> Large white paper
> Dowel
> Tape

Help your child cut two wide strips from red construction paper. Draw or trace a maple leaf onto red construction paper and help your child cut it out. Glue the red strips and maple leaf onto a piece of white paper to make a Canadian flag. Tape the flag to a dowel and fly the flag proudly!

Thanksgiving Day

While it is traditional to celebrate the harvest with a huge meal of roast turkey and all the trimmings, this year try to emphasize the "giving" in Thanksgiving. Talk with your child about all that you have for which you are thankful. This is an ideal time to share your wealth with others and to encourage a giving spirit in your child. Consider the following activities: Collect food in your neighbourhood and take it to a local food bank; do some special baking and take it to a nursing home or to a housebound neighbour; take some good, usable clothing and toys to a local relief agency; invite someone who is alone to share your Thanksgiving celebration.

PAPER PLATE TURKEY

Paper plate
Brown paint or crayon
Construction paper in various colours
Glue or paste
Markers or crayons

Have your child colour a paper plate with brown paint or crayon. Cut feathers out of coloured construction paper and glue them to the edge of the plate. Cut out a head, a neck, and feet, and glue them to the plate. Draw a turkey face with markers or crayons.

THANKSGIVING PLACE MAT

Old magazines
Construction paper or light cardboard
Glue or paste
Clear contact paper

Give your child old magazines and have him cut out things for which he is thankful. Let him glue them onto a piece of cardboard or construction paper. Cover the artwork with clear contact paper to create a Thanksgiving place mat.

THANKSGIVING CAN

Index cards or small pieces of paper
Old magazines (optional)
Glue or paste
Empty coffee can

Several weeks before Thanksgiving, ask your child to tell you for what he is thankful. On index cards or strips of paper, write down what he tells you. (Or have your child search through old magazines for appropriate pictures he can cut out and glue onto index cards.) Place the cards inside an empty coffee can. At bedtime, breakfast, or quiet time, have your child reach into the can and remove one card, then talk about what is on the card and why he is thankful for it.

THANKSGIVING PLACE CARDS

Yellow construction paper
Brown liquid tempera paint
Pen or marker

Fold a piece of yellow construction paper in half. Dip your child's palm into brown liquid tempera paint and carefully print it on the paper. When the paint dries, make the print look like a turkey: Use a pen or marker to add legs, an eye, a beak, and a wattle (the folds of loose red flesh under a turkey's throat). Print a name next to the turkey and use it on the Thanksgiving dinner table as a place card.

THANKSGIVING TREE

Construction paper in fall colours
Poster board or cardboard
Scissors
Markers
Glue or paste
Old catalogues or magazines (optional)

Cut leaf shapes out of coloured construction paper. You can draw the shapes on paper and have your child cut them out, or make a leaf pattern your child can trace himself. Draw a tree trunk and branches on a piece of cardboard or poster board. Ask your child to name things for which he is thankful and write them on each leaf (or use pictures cut from old magazines or catalogues). Have your child glue the leaves or pictures onto the branches. Display the tree in a prominent place as a reminder of your many blessings.

Halloween

While many people choose to celebrate Halloween without its traditional ghoulish emphasis, this holiday still provides an excuse for a good costume party. Our family activities vary from year to year. Sometimes we dress in fun, non-scary costumes, carve a pumpkin with a big, happy face, and attend a party with a "Fall Carnival" theme where we eat, play games, and come home with enough candy to last six months. Other years we have opted for smaller get-togethers, and one year we skipped the night altogether and went away for the weekend.

Regardless of how you celebrate this occasion, here are some fun activities for you and your child to try.

PoM PoM SPIDER

> Black yarn
> Small square of cardboard
> Scissors
> Black pipe cleaners
> Googly eyes (optional)
> Red construction paper (optional)
> Glue (optional)

Wind black yarn around a small square of cardboard, top to bottom, until the cardboard is very heavily and snugly covered. Tie a small piece of yarn securely around the middle of the yarn and the cardboard. (This piece should be tied fairly tightly, but not knotted, as it will be tightened after the cardboard is removed.) Using scissors, cut the yarn horizontally at both ends of the cardboard. Remove the cardboard, then tighten and knot the piece of yarn in the middle; it now forms the centre of the pom-pom. Insert three pipe cleaners into the knotted centre, and bend to form legs. You may have to trim the yarn to form a nice, even ball. Glue on googly eyes, if you like, or cut eyes out of red construction paper and glue them onto the pom-pom. Use thread or yarn to hang your spider from the doorway or in the window.

EGG CARTON SPIDER

> Cardboard egg carton
> Black tempera paint, markers, or crayons
> Scissors
> Black pipe cleaners
> Red construction paper
> Glue
> Thread or yarn

Using paint, marker, or crayon, colour the cup sections of an egg carton. If using paint, wait until the paint dries, then cut the egg cups apart. Push pipe cleaner legs into each egg cup and bend them so they look like spiders' legs. Cut red eyes from the construction paper and glue them onto the cups. Use thread or yarn to hang your spiders from the doorway or in the window.

HALLOWEEN CHAIN

> Scissors
> Black and orange construction paper
> Glue or paste

Here's a variation on the traditional Christmas tree decoration. Cut strips of black and orange construction paper, three to four inches long and one-half to one inch wide. Have your child form a circle with one strip, gluing the ends together. Take the next strip and loop it through the first circle, again gluing the ends together. Tell your child to continue looping and gluing to make a chain as long as he wants. Use the chain to decorate doorways, walls, windows, and so on.

BAKED PUMPKIN SEEDS

> Pumpkin seeds
> Cookie sheet
> Salt

As you prepare your Thanksgiving or Halloween pumpkin, save and dry the seeds. Spread dried seeds on a cookie sheet, salt and quickly broil them until lightly browned. Have your child count them into groups of two, three, four, and so on, before eating them.

GLOWING PUMPKIN DRAWING

> Construction paper
> Orange and black crayons
> Black (or other contrasting colour) tempera paint
> Paintbrush
> Varnish (optional)

Using crayons, help your child draw an outline of a pumpkin on a piece of construction or other paper. He should press hard, and fill in the outline with plenty of thick colouring. Then have him paint the picture with black (or other contrasting colour) tempera paint. Since wax repels water, the coloured areas will resist the paint and the painting will "glow". For a really dramatic effect, use fluorescent crayons, and finish with a coat of varnish.

Christmas

Christmas — a time when Christians the world over traditionally celebrate the birth of the baby Jesus, a time for peace on earth and goodwill to all men. But for our children (and ourselves), is Christmas really a time of peace and joy? As a child, the official start of Christmas for me was the arrival of the Sears Wish Book. As an adult, I know Christmas is on its way when stress levels rise, activity increases to frenzied proportions, and I become convinced that my home and family should look like the cover of the Sears catalogue!

We are easily caught up in the excitement of the season: the entertaining and partying, the cooking and baking, the shopping and wrapping. We are physically and emotionally and usually financially stretched to our limits. Sometimes we hold unrealistic expectations for ourselves and our family that only add to the stress. A four-year-old may easily wonder why such a special holiday leaves no time to read a book or go for a leisurely walk together.

At this busy time of year, concentrate on what is important. Relax and make time for your children and their simple pleasures. Go build a snowman, or read a story by the fire. Bake cookies together, or turn out the lights and watch the Christmas tree. Bundle up the family for a tour of your neighbourhood's Christmas lights, then come home to a mug of steaming cocoa. You probably won't look like the cover of the Sears catalogue, but together you will create traditions and make memories that will last a lifetime.

ACTIVITY ADVENT CALENDAR

Calendar or weekly planner

In the Christian tradition, Advent begins four Sundays before Christmas, but for this idea the beginning of December is also appropriate. Take out your weekly planner or your wall calendar and mark down a special activity to do with your child each day. For example: Stamp and mail your holiday greetings, make some gift-wrap together, bake and decorate Christmas cookies, or read a Christmas story by the fire. You can work a lot of your "to do" list into these activities, and planning something special for each day gives you one more way to count down the days to Christmas.

GRAHAM WAFER HOUSE

This "gingerbread" house is made with graham wafers and is easier for little hands than one made with traditional gingerbread.

Graham wafers
Cardboard milk carton
Ornamental Frosting (see Appendix A)
Gumdrops, candy, raisins, chocolate chips, Lifesavers, cereal, and
    other edible decorations

Make Ornamental Frosting (Appendix A) to hold the house together. Use the frosting to cement graham wafers to the sides of a cardboard milk carton (remember to cover the icing with a damp cloth when you're not using it). Allow the icing to set partially before adding the roof. Decorate with gumdrops, candies, raisins, chocolate chips, Lifesavers, cereal, and so on.

CANDY ADVENT CALENDAR

This activity continues to be a highlight in our family, and tends to mark the official start of our Advent celebrations. Stock up on your candy and supplies, and invite friends or family to make calendars with you.

> Red or green poster board (or construction paper glued to a file folder or piece of cardboard)
> Pen or marker
> Old Christmas cards, rubber stamps, or Christmas stickers
> Scissors (optional)
> Glue (optional)
> 25 pieces of wrapped Christmas candy
> Ornamental Frosting (see Appendix A)
> Hole punch
> Ribbon

Draw a December calendar on the bottom half of a piece of red or green poster board. Have your child cut designs from old Christmas cards and glue to the top half of the poster board, or decorate it with rubber stamps or Christmas stickers. Use Ornamental Frosting to stick a small piece of wrapped candy onto each grid of the calendar from December 1 through December 25. Lay the calendar flat until the icing sets, then punch a hole in the top and make a hanging loop of ribbon. Each day your child will have a visual and tasty reminder of the number of days until Christmas.

CHRISTMAS DOUGH ORNAMENTS

Make up a batch of dough ornaments (see Baker's Clay or No-Bake Cookie Clay recipes in Appendix A). Glue magnets to the backs for Christmas refrigerator decorations, hang from your Christmas tree as ornaments, give as Christmas gifts, or use as a finishing touch on wrapped gifts.

CHRISTMAS PLACE MATS

Used greeting cards
Scissors
Construction paper or light cardboard
Glue or paste
Clear contact paper

Cut up old greetings cards, glue artwork onto a piece of construction paper or light cardboard and cover with clear contact paper for a great Christmas place mat. As a variation, make a Christmas Wish-List Place Mat: Have your child cut out his gift wishes from an old Christmas catalogue or magazine and glue them onto a piece of construction paper. Cover the design with clear contact paper and use it as a place mat.

HOMEMADE GIFT-WRAP

This is a good activity for Christmas or any time of the year. Not only is it environmentally sound, but homemade gift-wrap is far more economical and personal than the commercially-bought wrap, and your child will love to make it, too.

Brown paper bags, butcher paper, or large sheets of plain paper
Rubber stamps
Ink pads

Cut open brown paper bags or use butcher paper or large sheets of other paper. Using rubber stamps and ink pads in a variety of colors, your child can decorate the paper according to his personal taste. The colours and rubber stamps can be varied according to the season or occasion.

PAPER SNOWFLAKES

White tissue paper cut into squares
Scissors

Fold a square piece of white tissue paper into quarters, then fold into a triangle shape. Cut small shapes along the folded edges, then unfold it to see a snowflake. Tape the snowflake to your window, or around the house for some holiday decorating.

CHRISTMAS COUNTDOWN

    25 small candy canes, individual pieces of candy, or candy kisses (for each child)
    One bowl, candy dish, or empty coffee can (for each child)

Place 25 small candy canes, kisses, or other special candy treats into a bowl, candy dish, or empty coffee can. Beginning December 1, let your child have one treat from his bowl every day. When he begins to ask "How many days 'til Christmas?" (and he will!) he can see for himself by counting the number of candies left in the bowl.

CHRISTMAS GIVING

    Small toy or gift
    Gift-wrap
    Tape

Help your child understand the true meaning of Christmas giving. Take him with you to buy a toy or gift for a local charity. Help him wrap it, then deliver it together. On your way home, stop for a muffin or hot chocolate.

DIP & DYE SNOWFLAKES

    Cone or square-shaped coffee filters or paper towels cut in circles or squares
    Small bowls of dye (diluted food colouring or strong tempera paint)
    Scissors

Fold coffee filters or paper-towel circles or squares in half, quarters, thirds, and so on. Dip into a bowl of dye, blot, open up, and let dry. When dry, fold again and make snowflakes by cutting small shapes along the folded edges. Use the snowflakes as a holiday decoration; tape to your window or your child's bedroom door.

CHRISTMAS CLOVES

Cloves
Orange

Push the pointy ends of the cloves into an orange. Make sure the cloves are firmly attached. The thick ends of the cloves will keep them from being pushed in all the way. Try to keep the cloves' depth as uniform as possible. Cover the entire orange with cloves and enjoy the Christmas scent.

HOLIDAY COOKIES

Rolled cookie dough
Christmas cookie cutters
Coloured icing
Sprinkles or other decorative candy

This is one Christmas activity that my sisters and I looked forward to all year. Make a batch of Cookie Cut-outs (Chapter 3), sugar cookies, or other rolled dough cookies. Use Christmas cookie cutters to cut out angels, Christmas trees, bells, and so on. After the cookies have been baked and cooled, set your child up at the table with bowls of icing in various colours and all kinds of little goodies for decorating: sprinkles, raisins, chocolate chips, gumdrops, and so on. He will probably eat more than he decorates, but this will become a well-cherished memory.

GLITTER BALLS

Styrofoam balls in various sizes
Glue
Glitter
Two small shallow dishes
Paintbrush
Thread

Pour glue and glitter into two separate shallow dishes. Use a paintbrush to spread glue evenly over a Styrofoam ball, then roll it in glitter. Allow the ball to dry, then attach a thread for hanging on the Christmas tree.

CHRISTMAS TREE PICTURE

Construction paper in green and other colours
Scissors
Hole punch
Glue
Sequins or glitter

Cut out a Christmas tree from green construction paper. Use a hole punch to punch out dots from various colours of construction paper. Glue the dots to your tree for decorations; add sequins or glitter and a star at the top.

PHOTO ORNAMENTS

Photograph of your child
Construction paper or cardboard
Scissors
Tape
Glue
Hole punch
Yarn

Draw a star on construction paper, or cut one out of cardboard and let your child trace it onto the paper. Cut it out. You will need two stars for each ornament. Cut an opening in the middle of one paper star and place your child's photo behind it. Trim the photo to fit, and tape it to the back of the star. Dab glue onto the back edges of the star, and press the second paper star onto it. Punch a hole at the top and thread yarn through; tie it to form a hanger for your ornament. Write your child's name and age on the back; he will be proud to hang it on the tree, year after year.

JINGLE BELLS

Bells
Ribbon or narrow elastic

Show your child how to string several bells onto a piece of ribbon or elastic to make a bracelet, or string bells onto your child's shoelaces. Sing "Jingle Bells" as your child jingles through the house.

THANK-YOU CARDS

Construction or other paper
Markers or crayons
Stickers (optional)
Cookie cutters (optional)
Old Christmas cards (optional)
Scissors (optional)
Glue (optional)

Make thank-you cards in advance to help ensure they are sent out promptly when gifts are received. Fold a sheet of paper in half or quarters, and have your child decorate it with crayons or markers, or try some of these ideas:

Decorate the card with Christmas stickers.
Trace Christmas cookie cutters shapes.
Trace around your child's hand.
Cut up and glue on old Christmas cards.
Rub a crayon sideways over a card with a raised design (see
    Christmas Rubbings).

CHRISTMAS RUBBINGS

Christmas card with a raised design
White paper
Crayons

Lay a piece of white paper over a Christmas card with a raised design on it. Your child can rub a crayon over the paper and watch the design appear.

REINDEER ANTLERS

Brown construction paper
Scissors
Glue

Cut a brown-construction-paper band to fit your child's head. Trace his handprints on the paper, cut them out and glue them to the headband as reindeer antlers.

CHRISTMAS CHAIN

Construction paper in red and green
Glue or paste

Cut strips of red and green construction paper, three to four inches long and one-half to one inch wide. Have your child form a circle with one strip, gluing the ends together. Take the next strip and loop it through the first circle, again gluing the ends together. Tell him to continue looping and gluing until the chain is the length he wants. Use the chain to decorate the Christmas tree, doorway, walls, and so on.

SNOW GLOBE

Small baby food jar with lid
Glue gun
Small toys or ornaments that fit into the jar
Water
Gold or silver glitter
¼ inch ribbon

Using the hot glue gun, glue ornaments or small toys to the inside of the lid of the jar; allow to dry. Have your child fill the jar with water, and add gold or silver glitter. Place the lid on the jar tightly and glue ribbon to the edge of the lid to seal it. Show your child how to shake up a snowstorm inside the jar.

CHRISTMAS CARD PUZZLES

Old Christmas cards
Heavy paper or cardboard
Glue
Scissors

Glue Christmas cards onto heavy paper or cardboard. When dry, cut into puzzles. The puzzle can be very simple and consist of only one card, or it can be more complicated, with two or more cards overlapping to make patterns and designs.

CHRISTMAS CARD HOLDER

Large green poster board
Small yellow poster board
Scissors
Large coloured clothespins or plastic paper clips
Glue
Ribbon
Hole punch
Heavy tape (optional)

Cut a green triangle and a yellow star out of poster board. Glue the star to the top of the green triangle. Glue paper clips or clothespins onto the green triangle Christmas tree. When dry, punch a hole through the poster board where the tree and star meet. Loop a ribbon through the hole and tie a knot. Hang on a hook on the wall, or use heavy tape to attach it to the refrigerator or your child's bedroom door. Attach the Christmas cards you receive to the paper clips or clothespins. (Try adapting this idea for other occasions: Make a Valentine holder by gluing clips onto a big heart cut from red poster board, or glue clips onto a large number "4" to hold cards from your child's fourth birthday.)

SNOWFLAKE WINDOW DECORATING

Square of plain or construction paper
Scissors
Tape
Can of spray-on artificial snow

Fold a square piece of paper into quarters, then fold it into a triangle shape. Cut small shapes along the folded edges, unfold, and tape the snowflake stencil to a window. Spray over the snowflake with artificial snow, then remove it to see the design on the window.

LOLLIPOP TREE

Bag of lollipops
Styrofoam cone
Scissors

Divide a bag of lollipops into three groups; one group will be used for the bottom of the tree, one for the middle, and one for the top. Set aside the group for the bottom; cut the sticks of the remaining groups medium length for the middle of the tree, and short for the top of the tree. Show your child how to poke the lollipops into a small Styrofoam cone to make a lollipop tree.

PAPER PLATE WREATH

> Green paper plate
> Red and green tissue paper
> Ribbon bow
> Scissors
> Glue

Cut a hole in the centre of a green paper plate. Cut or tear red and green tissue paper into small pieces. Have your child twist the paper or crumple into small balls and glue them onto the plate. Add a ribbon bow in a contrasting colour.

CHRISTMAS BELLS

> Egg carton
> Scissors
> Yarn, string, or ribbon
> Jingle bells
> Glue (optional)
> Glitter (optional)
> Paint (optional)
> Aluminum foil (optional)

Cut an egg carton into individual sections; paint, decorate with glitter, or cover with a small square of aluminum foil. Make a small hole in the top of each egg cup. Cut yarn, string, or ribbon into six-inch lengths and poke one end through the hole in the top of each egg cup. Thread the bottom piece of string through a jingle bell and back up through the hole at the top of the cup. Knot the ends. Hang on doorknobs (you may need a longer length of string) or on the tree as Christmas tree ornaments.

PAPER PLATE SNOWMAN

Cardboard or three small paper plates
Felt scraps
Glue
Cotton balls (optional)
Paint or markers
Stapler
Scissors

Cut three circles of increasing size from small paper plates or cardboard. Staple the circles together; one plate is the snowman's head and two make his body. Glue on cotton balls if you like. Cut out a scarf, buttons, features, and hat from felt scraps and glue them on. If you don't use cotton balls, paint the face with paint or markers, then glue on the accessories.

RICE KRISPIE SNOWMAN OR CHRISTMAS TREE

¼ cup margarine or butter
4 cups miniature marshmallows or 40 regular marshmallows
5 cups Rice Krispies
10 to 12 regular marshmallows
Toothpicks
Green food colouring (for tree)
Red cinnamon candies (for tree)
Shredded coconut (for snowman)
Candy for decoration (for snowman)

Melt margarine or butter in a large saucepan, then add 4 cups of marshmallows and cook over low heat, stirring constantly, until syrupy. Remove from heat. If making a Christmas tree, add green food colouring until the mixture is fairly dark green. Add Rice Krispies and stir until well coated.

To make Christmas trees, shape into conical forms with buttered hands. When the cones are cooled, stick a toothpick through a marshmallow and stick into the bottom to serve as the trees' base. Decorate with red candies.

To make snowmen, shape into small, medium and large balls and roll in coconut "snow". Join the balls with toothpicks and decorate with candies.

Hanukkah

Hanukkah, the most joyous and festive of all Jewish holidays, lasts eight days and takes place in December, sometimes early and sometimes late in the month.

Hanukkah, which means "dedication", was first celebrated more than 2,000 years ago. At that time, the Jewish people had just regained control of Judea, their homeland, after many years of repression by cruel foreign kings. Their beloved Temple of Jerusalem, the most important building in Jerusalem and a symbol of God's presence, was not fit for worship. The Jewish people worked hard to restore the Temple and make it pure and sacred once more. Finally it was ready for rededication, but only enough holy oil was found for the Temple menorah to burn for one day. The menorah was lit, the priests rededicated the Temple to God, and the people rejoiced. But their rejoicing was greater still when the oil lasted for eight days instead of one!

This is why Hanukkah is also called the Festival of Lights, and why the main focus of the celebration is the lighting of candles every day for eight days on the menorah, a special nine-branch candle holder. Every year Jews all over the world celebrate Hanukkah. Families gather to light the Hanukkah menorah, remember their ancestors' historic struggle for religious freedom, and recite blessings of thanks to God. Family members exchange gifts, eat special foods, play games, and retell the story of Hanukkah.

MENORAH

A Hanukkah menorah consists of nine candles, one for each day of Hanukkah, and one, called the shammash, used to light the other candles.

    9 empty thread spools
    Playdough
    Large birthday candles
    Aluminum foil (optional)

Make a Hanukkah menorah using empty thread spools to hold the candles. If the candles are a little loose, use some playdough to make them fit snugly. If you want to make the menorah more festive, cover the spools with aluminum foil.

Since a menorah can be any shape or size, use your imagination. Your preschooler can insert candles into playdough or modeling clay that he has shaped into a pleasing design. Try standing candles in a shoe box filled with sand, or drill holes for the candles in a tree branch or an interesting piece of driftwood.

Note: Traditionally, you should light your menorah every day and use new candles each time. You will need 44 candles in total for each menorah you light. Special packages of Hanukkah candles are available during this time of year. Each box contains all the candles you will need for one menorah.

STAR of DAVID NECKLACE

> Yellow, blue, and white construction paper
> Pencil or marker
> Ruler
> Glue
> Scissors

Draw two triangles (with two- to three-inch sides) on the yellow construction paper and have your child cut them out. Show him how to make a Star of David by turning one triangle upside down, placing it on top of the other, and gluing them together. Show your child how to make a chain with strips of white and blue construction paper (see Christmas Chain, this chapter). Glue the star to the chain to make a necklace or decoration.

DREIDEL

Dreidel is the name of both the small spinning top used to play this game and of the game itself. Follow these directions to make your own dreidel, then read on for some fun dreidel games.

> Small, square milk or juice carton
> Plain paper
> Tape
> Piece of ¼-inch dowel or unsharpened pencil
> Pen or marker

Flatten the top of the milk or juice carton and tape it securely. Cover the box with plain paper. On each side, write one of the Hebrew characters shown, or simply write the letters N, G, H and S. Push the dowel or pencil through from top to bottom and spin. (The Hebrew characters are the letters shin, heh, gimmel and noon. These are the first letters in the four words of the Hebrew message nes gadol hayah sham, read right to left, which means "A great miracle happened there.")

DREIDEL GAMES

    Homemade or store-bought dreidel
    Pennies, dried beans, raisins, or other tokens for each player

(1)   Each player puts one item from his pile of tokens into the centre, making a pile called the pot. The first player spins the dreidel; the letter that comes up determines what to do:

נ   (noon) or N – the player does nothing

ג   (gimmel) or G – the player takes the pot and everyone puts in one more item before the next player spins

ה   (heh) or H – the player takes half of the pot

ש   (shin) or S – the player puts one item into the pot.

When the pot is empty or only one token remains, every player puts one item in before the next player spins. The game is over when one player has won everything and everyone else has nothing.

(2)   Letters of the Hebrew alphabet also have number values, and older children may enjoy keeping score. Noon equals 50, gimmel is 3, heh is 5, and shin is 300. Each player in turn spins the dreidel and wins the number of points corresponding to the Hebrew letter that lands upright.

POTATO LATKES

Since oil was an important part of the Temple rededication, eating foods cooked in oil has come to symbolize the victory of the Jews over their enemies. This recipe will make about fifteen latkes (Yiddish for "pancake").

> 5 medium-sized potatoes
> 1 small onion
> 2 eggs, beaten
> 2 Tbsp. flour
> ¼ tsp. salt
> ¼ tsp. pepper
> Salad oil

Grate the potatoes and onion into a medium-sized bowl. Put the mixture into a sieve and press out the extra liquid. Add the beaten eggs to the potato/onion mixture. Add the flour, salt, and pepper and mix well. Pour about ¼-inch salad oil into the bottom of a large frying pan. Heat the oil, and keep it hot at medium to medium-high heat. Be careful — the oil will splatter. Put batter by the tablespoon into the oil and press each with a slotted spatula to make a thin pancake. When the edges get brown, turn the latke over and cook the other side until golden brown and crisp.

Serve warm with sour cream and applesauce.

HANUKKAH COOKIES

> Paper and pencil
> Scissors
> Rolled cookie dough
> Plastic knife

Make a batch of dough for Cookie Cut-Outs (Chapter 3), sugar cookies, gingerbread, or other rolled cookies. Chill. While the dough is chilling, draw some traditional Hanukkah shapes on paper and cut them out. Some shapes you can try are a Star of David (six-pointed star), a candle, a hammer (the Jews who recaptured their homeland were called Maccabees or "hammerers"), or an elephant (used by the Syrians in their battle with the Jews). Place the paper shapes on the rolled dough and cut around them with a knife. (Your preschooler will be able to cut around simple shapes with a plastic knife). Bake the cookies according to the recipe directions.

Appendix A

Basic Craft Recipes

Even at a very young age, your child can begin to develop his own creative skills and understand the artistic work of others. Visual art is not limited to paper and paint, but includes many different media. The craft materials in this chapter are essential for every child's artwork: paint, glue, paste, modeling compounds and more.

Paint

Each of the following recipes will produce a good paint for your child to use. Each varies in the ingredients required and the method used, so choose one that best suits the supplies you have on hand and the time you have available.

When mixing paint, keep in mind the age of the artist; as a general rule, the younger the artist, the thicker the paint (and brushes) should be. Paint should be stored covered; small plastic spill-proof paint containers are available at your local art supply store. These come with an air-tight lid for storage, hold brushes upright nicely without tipping, and at several dollars each are well worth the purchase price.

FLOUR-BASED POSTER PAINT

    ¼ cup flour
    1 cup water
    Powdered tempera paint
    Water
    Liquid starch or liquid detergent (optional)

Measure flour into a saucepan. Slowly add one cup water to make the paste smooth. Heat, stirring constantly, until mixture begins to thicken. Cool. Measure a quarter cup of the flour paste into small jars or plastic containers. Add 3 tablespoons powdered tempera paint and 2 tablespoons water for each colour. For an opaque finish, add liquid starch. For a glossy finish, add liquid detergent. Store covered.

DETERGENT POSTER PAINT

    1 Tbsp. clear liquid detergent
    2 tsp. powdered tempera paint

For each colour, mix together liquid detergent and powdered tempera paint in a small jar or plastic container. This makes enough for one painting session.

HOMEMADE FACE PAINT

This face paint is suitable for painting designs with a small brush.

    1 tsp. cornstarch
    ½ tsp. cold cream
    ½ tsp. water
    Food colouring

In a bowl, stir together the cornstarch and cold cream until well blended. Add water and stir. Add food colouring, one drop at a time until you get the desired colour. Paint designs on face with a small paintbrush; remove with soap and water. Store in a covered plastic container or a baby food jar.

HALLOWEEN FACE PAINT

This face paint is suitable for applying over a large area, such as an entire face.

> 1 Tbsp. solid shortening
> 2 Tbsp. cornstarch
> Food colouring

In a bowl, mix shortening and cornstarch together until smooth. Add food colouring, one drop at a time until you get the desired colour. Use a sponge or your fingers to apply paint over a large area such as an entire face. To paint a design with a small brush, thin the paint with a little water first. Remove with soap and water. Store paint in a baby food jar or covered plastic container.

CONDENSED MILK PAINT

> 1 cup condensed milk
> Food colouring

Mix one cup of condensed milk in a bowl with drops of food colouring to make a very glossy, brightly coloured paint. This paint is not intended to be eaten, but it won't harm any child who decides to make a snack of it.

EGG YOLK PAINT

This recipe is suitable for painting edible cookies.

> 1 egg yolk
> ¼ tsp. water
> Food colouring

In a bowl, mix one egg yolk with a quarter teaspoon water and lots of food colouring. Use a paint brush to paint on freshly baked cookies; return cookies to oven until egg solidifies.

Fingerpaint

Each of the following recipes produces a good fingerpaint, however the ingredients and mixing methods vary. Choose one that is suitable for the ingredients you have on hand and the time you have available.

CORNSTARCH FINGERPAINT

3 Tbsp. sugar
½ cup cornstarch
2 cups cold water
Food colouring
Soap flakes or liquid dishwashing detergent

Mix sugar and cornstarch in a medium saucepan over low heat. Add cold water and continue stirring until the mixture is thick. Remove from heat. Divide the mixture up into four or five portions, spooning them into sections of a muffin tin or small cups. Add a drop or two of food colouring and a pinch of soap flakes or a drop of liquid dishwashing detergent to each portion. Use a different colour for each cup. Stir and let cool. Store covered in an airtight container.

FLOUR FINGERPAINT

1 cup flour
2 Tbsp. salt
1½ cups cold water
1¼ cups hot water
Food colouring or tempera paint

Put flour and salt in a saucepan. Add cold water and beat with a whisk or rotary beater until smooth. Add hot water and boil until mixture is thick. Beat again until smooth. Keep in refrigerator and colour as needed with food colouring or powdered paint.

Playdough

Everyone seems to have their own favourite playdough recipe, and many old favourites have been included here. Some require cooking, some are no-cook, some are meant to be eaten, and some are not. Choose the recipe that best suits your requirements and the ingredients you have on hand. Store playdough in a covered container or plastic bag. If it sweats a little, just add more flour.

OATMEAL PLAYDOUGH

This is an ideal playdough for your child to make for herself. It needs to be refrigerated after making, and it doesn't last as long as cooked play-dough.

> 1 part flour
> 1 part water
> 2 parts oatmeal

Combine all ingredients in a bowl; mix well and knead until smooth. This is not intended to be edible playdough, but it will not hurt kids if they eat it.

UNCOOKED PLAYDOUGH

> 1 cup cold water
> 1 cup salt
> 2 tsp. vegetable oil
> Tempera paint or food colouring
> 3 cups flour
> 2 Tbsp. cornstarch

Mix the water, salt, oil, and enough tempera paint to make a bright colour. Gradually add flour and cornstarch until the mixtures reaches the consistency of bread dough.

PEANUT BUTTER PLAYDOUGH

Definitely an edible playdough!

  18 oz. peanut butter
  6 Tbsp. honey
  Non-fat dry milk or milk plus flour
  Optional: cocoa or carob for chocolate flavour

Combine all ingredients in a bowl and mix, adding enough dry milk or milk plus flour to reach the consistency of bread dough. Add cocoa or carob, if desired. Shape, decorate with other edible treats, and eat!

SALT PLAYDOUGH

  1 cup salt
  1 cup water
  ½ cup flour

Mix together and cook over medium heat. Remove from heat when mixture is thick and rubbery. As the mixture cools, knead in enough flour to make the dough workable.

COLOURED PLAYDOUGH

This playdough has a great consistency and lasts a long time.

  1 cup water
  1 Tbsp. vegetable oil
  ½ cup salt
  1 T. cream of tartar
  Food colouring
  1 cup flour

Combine water, oil, salt, cream of tartar, and food colouring in a saucepan and heat until warm. Remove from heat and add flour. Stir, then knead until smooth. Keep in mind that the cream of tartar makes this dough long-lasting—up to six months or longer—so resist the temptation to leave it out if you don't have it on hand. This dough should be stored in an airtight container or a zippered freezer bag.

Kool-Aid Playdough

½ cup salt
2 cups water
Food colouring, tempera powder, or Kool-Aid for colour
2 Tbsp. salad oil
2 cups sifted flour
2 Tbsp. alum (available at your grocery or drugstore)

Boil the salt in the water in a saucepan until salt is dissolved. Remove from heat and tint with food colouring, tempera powder, or Kool-Aid. Add salad oil, flour, and alum. Knead or process until smooth. This dough will last two months or longer.

Clay

Use the following recipes to produce clay which can be rolled or shaped into ornaments. The drying methods vary, either overnight or in the oven. When hard, ornaments can be painted and preserved with acrylic.

No-Bake Cookie Clay

These ornaments are not edible!

2 cups salt
⅔ cup water
1 cup cornstarch
½ cup cold water
Paint, glitter, and other decorative materials

Mix salt with ⅔ cup water in a medium saucepan. Stir and boil. Add cornstarch and ½ cup cold water and stir. If the mixture doesn't get thick, set it back on the stove. Sprinkle some extra cornstarch onto the table and a rolling pin. Roll out the dough with the rolling pin and cut with cookie cutters. Use a straw to make a hole at the top for hanging. Dry and decorate with paint, glitter, and so on.

NO-BAKE CRAFT CLAY

   1 cup cornstarch
   1¼ cups cold water
   2 cups baking soda (1 lb.)
   Food colouring (optional)
   Tempera paints or acrylic paints (optional)

Combine cornstarch, cold water, and baking soda in a saucepan; stir over medium heat for about four minutes until the mixture thickens to a moist mashed-potato consistency. For colour, add a few drops of food colouring to the water before it is mixed with the cornstarch and baking soda. Remove from heat, turn out onto a plate and cover with a damp cloth until cool. Knead as you would dough. Shape as desired or store in an airtight container or plastic bag. Objects may be left to dry then painted with tempera paints or acrylics. Dip in shellac, spray with clear acrylic, or brush with clear nail polish to seal.

MODELING CLAY

   2 cups salt
   ⅔ cups water
   1 cup cornstarch
   ½ cup cold water

Stir salt and water in a saucepan over heat four to five minutes. Remove from heat; add cornstarch and cold water. Stir until smooth; return to heat and cook until thick. Store in a plastic bag.

BREAD CLAY

   6 slices white bread, crusts removed
   6 Tbsp. white glue
   ½ tsp. detergent or 2 tsp. glycerine
   Food colouring

Knead the bread slices with glue plus either detergent or glycerine until the mixture is no longer sticky. Separate into portions and tint with food colouring. Let your child shape the clay. Brush the unfinished product with equal parts glue and water for a smooth appearance. Let dry overnight to harden. Use acrylic paints, acrylic spray, or clear nail polish to seal and preserve.

BAKER'S CLAY

4 cups flour
1 cup salt
1 tsp. powdered alum
1½ cups water
Food colouring (optional)

Mix all ingredients in a large bowl. If the dough is too dry, work in another tablespoon of water with your hands. Dough can be coloured by dividing it into several parts and kneading a drop or two of food colouring into each part. Roll or mould as desired.

To Roll: Roll dough one-eighth-inch thick on a lightly floured surface. Cut with cookie cutters dipped in flour. Make a hole in the top, a quarter inch down, for hanging, by using the end of a plastic straw dipped in flour. Shake the dots of clay from the straw and press on as decorations.

To Mould: Shape dough no more than half-inch thick into figures such as flowers, fruits, animals, and so on. Insert a fine wire in each for hanging.

Bake ornaments on an ungreased cookie sheet for about 30 minutes in a 250 degree oven. Turn and bake another one-and-a-half hours until hard and dry. Remove and cool, then sand lightly with fine sandpaper until smooth. Paint both sides with plastic-based poster paint, acrylic paint, or markers. Allow paint to dry and seal with clear shellac, acrylic spray, or clear nail polish.

Makes about 5 dozen two-and-a-half-inch ornaments.

Glue & Paste

The following glue and paste recipes use a variety of ingredients and methods. Choose the one that best suits your project. For variety, add food colouring to glue before using. Store all products in an airtight container in the refrigerator.

GLUE

¾ cup water
2 Tbsp. corn syrup
1 tsp. white vinegar
2 Tbsp. cornstarch
¾ cup cold water

Mix water, corn syrup, and white vinegar in a small saucepan. Bring to a full, rolling boil. In a small bowl, mix cornstarch with cold water. Add this mixture slowly to the hot mixture, stirring constantly until the mixture returns to a boil. Boil for one minute, then remove from heat. When slightly cooled, pour into another container and let stand overnight before using.

HOMEMADE PASTE

½ cup flour
Cold water

Add some cold water to the flour until it is as thick as cream. Simmer and stir in a saucepan for five minutes. Add a few drops of flavouring and/or food colouring, if desired. This makes a wet, messy paste that takes a while to dry.

NO-COOK PASTE

½ cup flour
Water
Salt

Mix the flour with water until gooey. Add a pinch of salt; stir.

PAPIER-MACHE PASTE

1 cup water
¼ cup flour
5 cups lightly boiling water

Mix flour into one cup of water until the mixture is thin and runny. Stir this mixture into the lightly boiling water. Gently boil and stir for two to three minutes. Cool before using.

other craft Recipes

Use the following recipes to make interesting materials for use in various art and craft projects.

COLOURFUL CREATIVE SALT

½ cup salt
5 to 6 drops food colouring

Add food colouring to salt and stir well. Cook in microwave for one to two minutes, or spread on wax paper and let air dry. Store in an airtight container. Use as you would glitter.

ORNAMENTAL FROSTING

This frosting works like an edible glue; use for gingerbread houses or other food projects that you want to eat!

3 egg whites
1 tsp. cream of tartar
1 lb. sifted icing sugar (about 4 cups)

Beat egg whites with cream of tartar in a bowl until stiff peaks form. Add sifted icing sugar and continue beating until mixture is thick and holds its shape. Cover with damp cloth when not in use. This can be made several hours or the day before using. Store in an airtight container in the refrigerator.

PASTA DYE

½ cup rubbing alcohol
Food colouring

Mix alcohol and food colouring in a bowl. Add small amounts of various dry pasta to the liquid and gently mix. The larger the pasta, the longer it will take to absorb the colour. Dry on newspapers covered with wax paper.

EGG DYE

¼ tsp. food colouring
¾ cup hot water
1 Tbsp. white vinegar

Measure all liquids into a bowl or cup and mix. Use different food colouring in each container for desired shades. Soak eggs in the dyes until they reach the desired shades.

Appendix B

Crazy Can Activities

The following activities are suitable for a Crazy Can (see Chapter 1). These activities are suggested because they require no special materials, need no time-consuming preparation or clean-up, and above all, demand a minimal amount of adult participation. Some of these ideas require a little advance planning (i.e., have a map or clues prepared in advance for the Indoor Treasure Hunt). These activities will provide you with an instant remedy when things start to get crazy, or when there's just "nothing to do." (The number following each activity refers to the page number on which that activity is found.)

Appendix C

Gifts for Kids to Make and Give

Most kids love to give gifts almost as much as they love to receive them, and the excitement is usually intensified if the gift is something they have made themselves. The following activities provide fun and easy ways for kids to personalize their gift-giving. The number following each activity refers to the page number on which that activity is found.

The following activities can be used to create unique and personal greetings cards and gift-wrap.

Best Books for Young Children

The following books are suggested for children up to age 8 (many are loved by much older children, too), either for reading by or to the child. This list has been compiled from several sources. *Timeless Classics,* published by the National Endowment for the Humanities, is a compilation of tried-and-true titles. These are books published in 1960 or before that have been the favourite of at least one previous generation. Another source is *Reading for the Love of It* by Michele Landsberg (1987, Prentice Hall Press / A division of Simon & Schuster, New York; reprinted by permission of the publisher), an excellent guide to the best books for children of all ages. A final source is the bookshelves in my own children's rooms, favourite volumes that have been read over and over and over again.

Aardema, Verna
  The Vingananee and the Tree Toad
  Why Mosquitoes Buzz in People's Ears

Aesop
  Aesop's Fables

Alderson, Sue Ann
  Bonnie McSmithers You're Driving Me Dithers

Allen, Jeffrey
  Mary Alice, Operator Number Nine

Ahlberg, Janet and Allen
Each Peach Pear Plum

Atwater, Richard and Florence
Mr. Popper's Penguins

Bemelmans, Ludwig
Madeline series

Brooke, Leslie L.
Johnny Crow's Party

Brown, Margaret Wise
Goodnight Moon

Brunhoff, Jean de
The Story of Babar

Burningham, John
Cannonball Simp
Harquin, the Fox Who Went Down to the Valley
Would You Rather?

Burton, Virginia Lee
Mike Mulligan and His Steam Shovel
The Little House

Caldicott, Randolph
Hey Diddle Diddle

Clifton, Lucille
Don't You Remember?

Crowther, Robert
The Most Amazing Hide-and-Seek Alphabet Book

Dalgleish, Alice
The Bears on Hemlock Mountain
The Courage of Sarah Noble

Eastman, P.D.
Are You My Mother?
Go, Dog, Go

Flack, Marjorie
The Story about Ping

Freeman, Don
Corduroy

Gag, Wanda
Millions of Cats

Godden, Rumer
The Mousewife

Goffstein, M.B.
Our Snowman

Grahame, Kenneth
The Reluctant Dragon

Haywood, Carolyn
Betsy series

Hoban, Russell
Bread and Jam for Frances

Hutchins, Pat
Rosie's Walk

Jonas, Ann
The Trek

Keats, Ezra Jack
Goggles!

Kellogg, Steven
The Island of the Skog

Kipling, Rudyard
Just So Stories for Little Children

Kovalski, Maryann
Brenda and Edward

Kraus, Robert
Herman the Helper
Whose Mouse Are You?

Leaf, Munro
The Story of Ferdinand

Lear, Edward
The Book of Nonsense

MacDonald, Betty
Mrs. Piggle-Wiggle

Marshall, James
George and Martha

McCloskey, Robert
Blueberries for Sal
Make Way for Ducklings

McDermott, Gerald
Papagayo, the Mischief-maker

Meyer, Mercer
Little Critter series

Milne, A.A.
The House at Pooh Corner
Now We Are Six
When We Were Very Young
Winnie-the-Pooh

Minaruk, Else Holmelund
Little Bear

Mosel, Arlene
The Funny Little Woman
Tikkie Tikki Tembo

Munsch, Robert
Love You Forever
The Paperbag Princess

Nicoll, Helen
Meg and Mog

Ormerod, Jan
Moonlight
Sunshine

Perrault, Charles
Cinderella

Pinkwater, Manus
Three Big Hogs

Potter, Beatrix
  The Tale of Peter Rabbit

Rey, H.A.
  Curious George series

Segal, Lore
  Tell Me a Mitzi
  Tell Me a Trudy

Selden, George
  The Cricket in Times Square

Sendak, Maurice
  Where the Wild Things Are

Seuss, Dr.
  Green Eggs and Ham
  The Cat in the Hat
  The 500 Hats of Bartholomew Cubbin

Shulevitz, Uri
  One Monday Morning

Steig, William
  Brave Irene
  Sylvester and the Magic Pebble

Stevenson, James
  Could Be Worse!

Stevenson, John
  Clams Can't Sing

Stevenson, Robert Louis
  A Child's Garden of Verses

Stamm, Claus
  Three Strong Women

Viorst, Judith
  Alexander and the Terrible, Horrible, No Good, Very Bad Day

Waber, Bernard
  Lyle the Crocodile series

Wagner, Jenny
The Bunyip of Berkeley's Creek

Wallace, Ian
Chin Chiang and the Dragon's Dance

Watson, Clyde
Applebet, an ABC

Wells, Rosemary
Noisy Nora

Wildsmith, Brian
Cat on the Mat

Williams, Jay
Everyone Knows What a Dragon Looks Like

Williams, Margery
The Velveteen Rabbit

Williams, Vera B.
Cherries and Cherry Pits

Wood, Audrey
Sid and Sol
The Napping House

Wynne-Jones, Tim
Zoom at Sea

Yeoman, John
The Wild Washerwoman

Yorinks, Arthur
Hey, Al

Zolotow, Charlotte
Mister Rabbit and the Lovely Present

Zemach, Harve
The Judge

Zion, Gene
Harry the Dirty Dog

Appendix E

Resources

This book is a combination of personal experience, contributions from friends and family, and ideas and information gathered from the books and government publications listed below.

Baby Games, Elaine Martin, Stoddart Publishing, 1988

Becoming a Nation of Readers: What Parents Can Do, D.C. Heath and Company and the U.S. Department of Education, 1988

Children's Art & Crafts, Nancy Lewis Bartlett, The Australian Women's Weekly Home Library, Australian Consolidated Press, 1991

Creative Family Times, Allen & Connie Hadidian, Will & Lindy Wilson, Moody Press, 1989

Dance and Your Child, The National Dance Association and The National Endowment for the Arts, 1991

Family Math, Stenmark, Thompson and Cossey, University of California, 1986 (For information contact: Lawrence Hall of Science, University of California, Berkeley, CA 94720, Attn: FAMILY MATH)

Feed Me! I'm Yours, Vicky Lansky, Meadowbrook Press, 1974

From Words to Stories, Teachers and Writers Collaborative and The National Endowment for the Arts, 1991

Hanukkah Book, The, Marilyn Burns, Fourwinds Press, 1981

Help! I Have a Pre-school Child!!!, Kandi Arnold, Andrea Devin, Dale Sprowl, Garborg's Heart 'N Home, 1990

Help Your Child Become a Good Reader, U.S. Department of Education

Helping Your Child Learn Geography, U.S. Department of Education, 1990

Helping Your Child Learn Math, U.S. Department of Education, 1993

Helping Your Child Learn to Read, U.S. Department of Education, 1993

Honey for a Child's Heart, Gladys Hunt, Zondervan, 1989

Jewish Holidays, Susan Gold-Purdy, J.B. Lipincott Company, 1969

Learning About Fall and Winter Holidays, Jeri A. Carroll and Candace B. Wells, Good Apple Inc., 1988.

Light Another Candle, Miriam Chaikin, Clarion Books, 1981.

Lollipop Grapes & Clothespin Critters, Robyn Freedman Spitzman, Addison-Wesley Publishing, 1985

Mother's Almanac, The, Marguerite Kelly & Elia Parsons, Doubleday, 1975

Mother's Manual for Summer Survival, A, Kathy Peel & Joy Mahaffey, Focus on the Family Publishing, 1989

Music and Your Child's Education, The Music Educators National Conference and The National Endowment for the Arts, 1991

Papier Mâché Artistry, Dona Z. Meilach, General Publishing, 1971

Prime Time Together ... With Kids, Donna Erickson, Augsburg Fortress, 1989

Rainy Day Activities for Preschoolers, Ann Marie Connolly & Helen Gibson, Mercer Island Preschool Association, 1988

Read-Aloud Handbook, The, Jim Trelease, Penguin Books, 1995

Reading for the Love of It, Michele Landsberg, Prentice Hall Press, 1987

Sunset Children's Crafts, Lane Publishing Co., 1976

Theater and Children, American Alliance for Theatre & Education and
   The National Endowment for the Arts, 1991

Timeless Classics, National Endowment for the Humanities, 1991

What To Do After You Turn Off The TV, Frances Moore Lappé, Random
   House, 1985

You Can Help Your Young Child Learn Mathematics, U.S. Department of
   Education, 1991

Your Baby & Child From Birth to Age Five, Penelope Leach, Random
   House, 1989

Your Child and the Visual Arts, The National Art Education Association
   and The National Endowment for the Arts, 1991

The United States General Services Administration makes available many
free and low-cost federal publications of consumer interest, including
many on learning activities and parenting. For a free catalogue write to:

Consumer Information Centre-2C
P.O. Box 100
Pueblo, Colorado
81002

T

ABOUT THE AUTHOR

Trish Kuffner lives with her husband, Wayne, and four children, Andria, Emily, Joshua, and Johanna, on an acreage in Coquitlam, just outside of Vancouver, B.C. After the birth of her second child in 1990, Trish left a demanding computer programming position to join the growing number of women choosing full-time motherhood over career.

Since the publication of the first edition of *Surviving Your Preschooler* in 1992, Trish has spoken to many parent and caregiver groups in British Columbia and Washington. She enjoys being a source of encouragement to others, and gives all the praise and glory to God for His unfailing love, mercy, grace, and leading in her life.

Trish is currently at work on producing both her second book, *Surviving Your Toddler,* and her fifth child – both projects are due to be completed in 1999. Trish and Wayne homeschool their four children.

Notes

Notes

Notes